OFSTED REVIEWS OF RESEARCH

Recent Research on the Achievements of Ethnic Minority Pupils

**David Gillborn
Caroline Gipps**

INSTITUTE OF EDUCATION
UNIVERSITY OF LONDON

LONDON: HMSO

ISBN 0 11 350084 X

Office for Standards in Education

Alexandra House

29 - 33 Kingsway

London WC2B 6SE

Telephone: 0171 421 6800

Facsimile: 0171 421 6707

DEDICATION

In 1996 the world of education lost one of its best researchers; we lost a good friend and colleague. This review is dedicated to the memory of Professor Barry Troyna.

CONTENTS

Tables

Figures

SUMMARY

The context for the review

- More than a decade has passed since the last major review of the educational experiences and achievements of ethnic minority pupils.

- In that time new findings and research methods have added to our understanding of the processes that affect pupils' educational performance.

- The same period has seen massive reforms of the education system that touch all those involved in education (including headteachers, governors, classroom teachers, parents and pupils).

- During this period, issues of race and equal opportunity have tended to slip from policy agendas: this review demonstrates the need for this to change.

Achievement

- This review focuses on differences in levels of achievement between different ethnic groups; we also consider the influence of factors such as social class and gender.

- 'Under-achievement' is a relatively crude term, relating to differences in group averages. It has long been misunderstood as implying that some groups are better or worse than others.

- Where there are significant differences in performance, we interpret this as a cause of concern, highlighting areas where minority pupils might face additional unjustifiable barriers to success.

Achievement in the early key stages

- Research on the performance of infant and junior school pupils does not paint a clear picture: on average African Caribbean pupils appear to achieve less well than whites, although the situation is reversed in recent material from Birmingham.

- A more consistent pattern concerns the lower average attainments of Bangladeshi and Pakistani pupils in the early key stages: this may reflect the significance of levels of fluency in English, which are strongly associated with performance at this stage.

Achievement at the end of compulsory education

- Performance in GCSE examinations at 16 can be vital to young people's future educational and employment chances. Results show that, regardless of ethnic origin, pupils from more economically advantaged backgrounds achieve the highest averages. Girls also tend to do rather better than boys from the same social class background.

- Recent years have seen widespread improvements in average GCSE performance. However, not all pupils have shared equally in this trend.

- In many LEAs the gap between the highest and lowest achieving groups has increased.

- There are no up-to-date nationally representative figures on GCSE performance by different ethnic groups. However, our review of research and new LEA data has identified some common patterns.

- Indian pupils appear consistently to achieve more highly, on average, than pupils from other South Asian backgrounds.

- Indian pupils achieve higher average rates of success than their white counterparts in some (but not all) urban areas.

- There is no single pattern of achievement for Pakistani pupils, although they achieve less well than whites in many areas.

- Bangladeshi pupils are known on average to have less fluency in English, and to experience greater levels of poverty, than other South Asian groups. Their relative achievements are often less than those of other ethnic groups. In one London borough, however, dramatic improvements in performance have been made - here Bangladeshis are now the highest achieving of all major ethnic groups.

- African Caribbean pupils have not shared equally in the increasing rates of educational achievement: in many LEAs their average achievements are significantly lower than other groups.

- The achievements of African Caribbean young men are a particular cause for concern.

- In some areas there is a growing gap between the achievements of African Caribbean pupils and their peers.

Educational progress and school effectiveness

- 'Progress' is a central concept in school effectiveness research; it refers to changes in performance over time, not to the final level of achievement.

- Achievement and progress are not the same: it is possible for a group to make relatively greater progress, yet still emerge with lesser qualifications (if they started with lower previous attainments).

- 'Multi-level modelling' is a statistical procedure that attempts to unravel the different elements that might affect pupils' performance, including social class, gender and ethnic origin.

- Judgements about 'effective' schools are made by comparing a school's predicted performance (based on the composition of its pupil population) and its real performance.

- The possibility of measuring a school's effect on performance ('the value added') is widely seen as a useful tool - unfortunately, some approaches lack rigour and may give misleading results.

Differences in educational progress

- Social class is strongly associated with differences in pupil progress.

- The higher rates of unemployment among some ethnic minority groups may have important educational consequences.

- In primary schools over time the gap widens between the performance of pupils from different social class backgrounds.

- Whites tend to make greater progress than ethnic minority pupils in primary schools.

- In secondary schools Asian pupils make rather better progress than whites of the same social class background. The performance of African Caribbean pupils is less consistent.

- Despite the greater progress made by some ethnic minority groups, studies outside London tend to show white pupils leaving school with the highest average achievements.

Research on school effectiveness and 'value added'

- The largest proportion of schools seem to be performing at roughly the predicted level (neither exceptionally effective nor ineffective).

- The idea of 'overall effectiveness' has been criticized: it may obscure changes over time (the issue of stability) and large variations in the effectiveness of subject departments within individual secondary schools (the issue of consistency).

- Some schools are especially effective for certain groups but relatively ineffective for others (this is known as 'differential effectiveness').

- Research suggests that some secondary schools are especially effective for certain ethnic groups - though the size and reasons for this remain largely unexplored.

- The composition of secondary schools might affect progress where there is an unusually large proportion of higher - or lower - achieving pupils. However, no 'compositional effects' have been found in relation to schools' ethnic balance of pupils.

Behind the numbers: qualitative research in multi-ethnic schools

- 'Qualitative' research tries to understand what participants think and examine the consequences of their interactions during the day-to-day routine of school life.

- The most common forms of qualitative research use interviews and observations. 'Ethnographic' studies involve long periods of research in a small number of schools. This research has produced important findings, but generalization is difficult because 'so few cases' have been studied.

- Like all social science data, qualitative evidence is open to multiple interpretations; researchers usually try to strengthen their analyses by drawing on several different types of material.

Racial violence and harassment

- Qualitative studies highlight the widespread incidence of racial harassment against some pupils.

- Racist harassment is not always recognised as such by teachers, who may mistakenly view it as simple boisterousness.

- Asian pupils seem especially likely to be victimized by their white peers. This echoes the pattern in society more generally and points to the urgent need for action against racial violence and harassment.

Exclusions from school

- Statistics indicate that exclusion from school is being used with increasing frequency. Exclusion is the most serious punishment available to headteachers: two out of every three pupils who are permanently excluded never return to full-time mainstream education.

- African Caribbean pupils are between three and six times more likely to be excluded than whites of the same sex: a pattern that is true for boys and girls in both primary and secondary schools.

- Qualitative research documents individual cases where pupils and their families feel that racial discrimination has occurred. In the future, qualitative research could offer a way of exploring whether issues of ethnicity are involved (directly or indirectly) in the wider use of exclusions at the school level.

Ethnic origin and teacher/pupil interactions

- Research in infant, primary and secondary schools has recorded an unusually high degree of conflict between white teachers and African Caribbean pupils.

- School case studies describe processes where, despite their best intentions, teachers' actions can create and amplify conflict with African Caribbean pupils.

- In comparison with African Caribbeans, teachers often have more positive expectations of Asians - as relatively quiet, well behaved and highly motivated.

- South Asian pupils are sometimes subject to negative and patronising stereotypes - especially concerning language abilities and the nature of their home communities.

- These stereotypes can be especially damaging for Asian girls.

Understanding success: qualitative perspectives

- In relation to the high achievements of certain ethnic minority pupils, existing research suggests that social class, gender and ethnic origin may all play an important role; unfortunately, the relative significance of these factors is not always clear.

- Some ethnic minority pupils respond negatively to school; this is sometimes seen as a means of resisting perceived injustices. Others adapt differently, seeing achievement as a sign of their worth and independence.

- Research suggests that a combination of gender- and race-specific stereotypes might make success especially difficult for African Caribbean young men.

- Qualitative research documents the long, uncertain and sometimes painful processes of change in schools.

- Case studies of primary and secondary schools highlight the potential for school-based change that involves teachers, pupils and local communities in a positive re-evaluation of the role and work of schools in a multi-ethnic society.

Post compulsory education

'Staying on': educational participation between 16 and 19

- Recent years have seen dramatic increases in the number of young people 'staying on' in education beyond the age of 16.

- This trend reflects several factors, in particular the shrinking youth labour market and the increasing level of GCSE achievements.

- It has long been known that young people from ethnic minority backgrounds tend to remain in full time education more often than their white counterparts. Participation in post compulsory education is higher for all major ethnic minority groups than for the white group.

- This pattern continues throughout the first three years of post compulsory education and, with virtually no exceptions, is true regardless of gender and social class background.

- The participation of Asian young people is especially high; even three years after the end of compulsory schooling, a majority of Asians are still in full time education.

- The reasons for the greater participation of ethnic minority young people are not clear. Among the possible explanations are greater motivation and parental support, and attempts to avoid unemployment and to off-set the impact of racism.

- Asian young people tend to follow traditional 'academic' courses. Consequently, by age 18 Asians are the most highly qualified of all groups (including whites).

- African Caribbean young people are more likely to follow vocational courses.

Access to Higher Education

- There is little reliable information on ethnic minority achievements within higher education; the point of entry, however, is now monitored for possible bias.

- Relatively more people of ethnic minority origin apply to enter Higher Education.

- Whites are more likely than their ethnic minority peers to be accepted by the 'old' universities; Black Caribbean and African applicants are accepted least often.

- Even when previous achievement is taken into account, people do not share an equal chance of admission; being male, attending a selective school and having parents in professional/managerial occupations all increase the probability of success.

- Taking all these factors into account, it is still the case that certain ethnic minority groups experience significantly different rates of admission to university: Chinese young people are more likely to be admitted than other groups; Black Caribbeans and Pakistanis are less likely to gain a place at university.

1 Introduction

It is now more than ten years since the publication of the final report of the Committee of Inquiry into the Education of Children from Ethnic Minority Groups - widely known as the 'Swann Report'.

In the intervening years, new research techniques have been devised and recent data have shed light on issues that were poorly understood a decade ago. However, the question of race and equality of opportunity has fallen from the prominent position it once held. This review, therefore, offers an important chance to take stock of recent changes in the educational achievements of ethnic minority pupils.

Differences in the age structures of minority communities are such that the number and proportion of people from ethnic minority backgrounds will grow in the future: it is estimated that by the year 2020 the minority population will have doubled[1].

One of the clearest findings of this review is that if ethnic diversity is ignored, if differences in educational achievement and experience are not examined, then considerable injustices will be sanctioned and enormous potential wasted.

The shape and style of the review

In a review of this size, it is not possible to include every piece of research or every area of concern. We have chosen to focus on issues that directly influence pupils' achievements, especially where they relate to education policy, schools and matters that teachers might wish to address as part of their work. Wherever possible we have tried to avoid jargon and to explain clearly any necessary technical terms. The review is broken into several sections:

Section 2: *looks at the achievement of ethnic minority pupils at different points in their educational careers, focusing in particular on the issue of 'under-achievement'.*

Section 3: *explores research on educational progress and school effectiveness.*

Section 4: *examines research on the day-to-day experiences of teachers and pupils in multi-ethnic schools.*

Section 5: *considers recent trends among young people who stay in full time education beyond age 16 (post compulsory).*

The review ends by considering briefly some of the major implications of our findings for future research, policy and practice.

Who's who? Some problems and definitions

According to the 1991 census, about 5.5 per cent of the British population are of 'ethnic minority' background. In theory the census invites people to make their own decisions about which ethnic category they belong to; in practice, they face a limited choice between categories that combine colour and national references. In the real world, the same person might choose to describe themselves differently (as say, Pakistani, Black, Asian or Muslim) depending on the particular context. Although common-sense understandings of 'race' tend to assume some sort of fixed, biological reference point, in fact people's ideas about the meaning of race and/or ethnic origin are constantly shifting. Witness the rapidly changing terminology that is used by, about and against different groups. This often hinders comparison between different research projects; arguments continue about the use of the term 'black', for example, and many people with family roots in the Indian subcontinent now reject the generalized use of the label once common among researchers[2].

In preparing this review, we have tried to indicate how different projects have categorized people. For our own purposes we have tried to describe people in terms they would recognize and accept. The following brief explanations may be useful:

- *'ethnic minority':* following common practice we use this as a general label for all people who would not define themselves as 'white' in terms of their ethnic identity[3];

- *Black:* may include individuals who would appear in census statistics as either Black Caribbean, Black African or Black Other. For certain calculations we combine the categories 'Black Caribbean' and 'Black Other'[4]. Where research distinguishes between Caribbean and African we have usually retained the distinction;

- *African Caribbean:* many people now consider this a more acceptable term than the categories 'Afro-Caribbean' and 'West Indian' that appear in older research. Where possible we use 'African Caribbean';

- *South Asian:* sometimes used as a general term to include people of Bangladeshi, Indian and Pakistani ethnic origin. Where possible, we distinguish between these groups, since they have different social, economic and cultural profiles;

- *Mixed race:* usually applied to children where only one of the natural parents is white. They are usually lost within statistical research (added to one of the other ethnic groups). Qualitative research (using interviews and observations) has given rather limited attention to this group[5].

NOTES TO SECTION 1

1   Runnymede Trust (1994, p.16).

2   Modood (1992) and Modood, Beishon and Virdee (1994).

3   Runnymede Trust (1994, p. 10).

4   Ballard and Kalra (1994) and Runnymede Trust (1994, p. 10).

5   Tizard and Phoenix (1993) and Wilson (1987).

2 Achievement

Debates about ethnic diversity in the English educational system have focused mainly on questions of achievement and under-achievement. In this section of the review, we begin by examining the concept of 'under-achievement' and go on to consider evidence on the relative achievement of minority pupils during the early stages of their compulsory education. Finally we explore research on pupils' achievements at the end of their compulsory schooling.

2.1 ACHIEVEMENT AND UNDER-ACHIEVEMENT

During the 1970s and 1980s, the issue of 'under-achievement' dominated debates about the education of ethnic minority pupils. In 1974 the Assessment of Performance Unit (APU) was set up within the Department for Education and Science (DES): one of its central objectives was to 'identify the incidence of under-achievement'[1].

In practice the APU looked for under-achievement by comparing the average performance of pupils in different groups. Hence the APU followed prominent practice in the United States where judgements about equality of *opportunity* were made by comparing the relative outcomes achieved by different groups[2]. This method of analysis has been hotly contested by some critics. It rests on the assumption that ability is randomly distributed, so that no social class or ethnic group is assumed to be inherently more intelligent than another. Although controversial debates about intelligence and genetics resurface periodically, most research in this country maintains a concern for relative achievement as an important means of monitoring for inequalities[3].

In this way, under-achievement refers to differences in the average attainments of different groups: it says nothing about the specific potential or achievements of any individual pupil.
The concept is useful for identifying potential causes for concern, areas where certain groups may not enjoy equal opportunities: only further investigation, however, can explain the factors that lie behind the statistics.

The notion of under-achievement came to particular prominence in this country through the work of the Committee of Inquiry into the Education of Children from Ethnic Minority Groups - chaired successively by Anthony Rampton and Lord Swann. The committee was set up in 1979 in response to widespread concerns about the academic performance of 'West Indian' pupils. By comparing the achievements of different ethnic groups the committee came to the conclusion that 'West Indian children *as a group* are under-achieving in our education system'[4]. There has been widespread misunderstanding of this conclusion, pointing to important weaknesses in the concept of under-achievement. For example, it has been argued that because teachers perceive 'black under-achievement' to be a national problem beyond their control, they might lower their expectations of certain pupils, creating a negative stereotype that effectively closes down opportunities[5]. Abstracting one or two particular measures of achievement and elevating them to a dominant status will necessarily lead to simplification. A study of eighteen multi-ethnic comprehensives in the 1980s, for example, found that *overall*, black pupils did not achieve as highly as their white and Asian peers - yet they were the single most successful group in English language examinations[6].

Conscious of these problems, we do not generally refer to *'under-achievement'* in this review. We prefer instead to focus on the *relative* achievements of pupils in different ethnic groups, conscious that total equality of outcome may be neither possible, nor just - for instance, if some ethnic groups have better attendance records, tend to spend longer on their homework and are more highly motivated (as some black and Asian groups appear when given questionnaire-based assessments), we might expect them to do better than less motivated groups[7]. Reliable information on such differences is scarce. Our position is that, in practice, *significant differences in the relative achievements of different ethnic groups may reasonably be taken as a cause for concern.* In reviewing the available evidence, attention will be drawn to discrepancies between the relative performance of different ethnic groups. Where differences are significant it is likely that the lower achieving group does not enjoy equal educational opportunities; they may face additional barriers that prevent them fulfilling their potential.

2.2 ACHIEVEMENT IN THE EARLY KEY STAGES

The ILEA Junior School Study, *School Matters,* reported comprehensive research on the performance of 2,000 pupils in 50 London junior schools from 1980 to 1984[8]. Children's performance was assessed on entry and in each of the following three years. Although the data are now rather old, the study remains important because it used a detailed breakdown of ethnic group, looked at both achievement and progress, and examined performance using a number of different cognitive and non-cognitive indices - including separate analyses for reading and writing attainments.

At the end of junior school, children who were not fully fluent in English, according to their classteacher, obtained markedly lower scores in reading than those who were fully fluent; furthermore, they had made significantly poorer progress over the three years.

Both ethnic background and language fluency had a statistically significant impact upon reading progress; children of Caribbean backgrounds and those of Asian origin made significantly poorer progress than other groups.

There was no significant relationship between ethnic background and *writing* performance on entry to junior school, although fluency in English was linked to both length and quality of writing. By the summer of the third year, pupils of Asian, Caribbean and Turkish background tended to produce shorter pieces of work. However, there were no significant differences between ethnic groups in terms of the quality of ideas, nor the quality of writing.

Maths attainment at entry to school was clearly related to ethnic background and fluency in English.

By the third year of the study, Caribbean children's attainment was the furthest below the average; Turkish and Greek children achieved a little better than the Caribbeans, while Asian Gujerati speaking pupils (a small group) scored above the average. There was no evidence that ethnic differences or fluency had any effect on progress in mathematics.

Differences in the performance of children from different ethnic backgrounds did not increase over the junior years in maths, in the way they did for reading.

The research found no relationship between teachers' ratings of pupils' ability and the children's ethnic background, once account had been taken of social class. Ability ratings were strongly related to pupil attainment - which were lower in reading, writing and maths for Caribbean and some Asian pupils. This suggests that for pupils from all ethnic backgrounds teachers' expectations were tied to specific knowledge of previous attainment and performance in the classroom. There was, however, some variation in teacher behaviour towards pupils of different ethnic origins. For example, teachers heard Caribbean pupils read more often, devoted more time to non-work contacts with them, and gave them more neutral and negative feedback on their behaviour than other groups. More recent school-based research also tends to show teachers controlling and criticizing black pupils more frequently than other groups[9].

A follow up of this sample, in General Certificate of Secondary Education (GCSE) examinations, found that the patterns of ethnic differences evident amongst younger age groups were not stable over the longer term. Although ethnic minority groups attained less highly during the junior phase of education (both in absolute and relative terms) these patterns altered during secondary education[10].

A second cohort of pupils (277 African Caribbean and white children in 33 London schools), born five years later than the *School Matters* cohort, was studied on entry to, and throughout, infant school[11]. Ethnic group differences were also studied at the end of junior school[12]. There were very few differences on entry to infant school except girls' superiority in writing.

By the end of infant school, African Caribbean girls had made the most- and African Caribbean boys the least progress in reading and writing.

Boys, particularly white boys, made more progress than girls in maths. By the end of junior school (in 1989), the gap between black girls and black boys in reading was maintained but did not widen, and boys' advantage over girls in maths was reduced. This cohort of pupils has the limitation of being only from inner-city London schools - with a narrower range of social class than the *School Matters* cohort, although all the children were fluent English speakers on entry to school. The African Caribbean boys were the lowest performing group.

A more recent study of a similar sample of Key Stage 1 pupils (in the same schools as the original infant school study) was undertaken to estimate the impact of the National Curriculum[13].

The African Caribbean pupils in this study had lower attainment in maths at the end of Year One and as a result tended to cover less of the curriculum in their second year. There was also evidence of a widening gap between black and white children at the end of Year Two[14].

Unfortunately, this phase of the study does not appear to carry social class data, making generalisation from the findings difficult.

By contrast, *monitoring in Birmingham LEA indicates that African Caribbean children do better than their peers in the basic skills throughout infant school,* as shown by assessments at the age of five and seven. This is in marked contrast to the GCSE performance of Birmingham's African Caribbean pupils aged 15-16[15]. In their baseline assessment programme, Birmingham teachers assess four and five year olds' basic skills, during normal classroom activities in their first term of reception class. In 1994, 4.6 per cent of African Caribbean young children performed at the levels expected of 6 or 7 year olds, compared with 3.6 per cent of white children[16].

The national assessment results at Key Stage 1 showed that in 1992 and 1994 black children were ahead of white children in Birmingham.

Performance at 7 was generally lower for pupils whose first language was not English[17]. A local authority spokesperson suggested that high expectations from parents, and the popularity of Saturday schools for black children, were contributing factors to their success. The Birmingham data have received a good deal of publicity, but the pattern is not repeated elsewhere. The London Borough of Wandsworth also carries out baseline assessment at age 4+. Over the three years 1992/93 to 1994/95, the average standardised score for 'Caribbean' pupils (96.4) was below the national average; however, this reflects the somewhat poorer performance of Caribbean boys (92.5 compared with 99.9 for Caribbean girls). Boys of Pakistani, Bangladeshi and Chinese ethnic origin also achieved consistently less well[18].

National assessment results at Key Stage 1

An evaluation of the summer 1991 tests examined the performance of a sample of children within 17 LEAs. Teacher assessment results, the Standard Assessment Task (SAT) results and additional detailed assessments of the children's achievements were collected from an overall sample of more than 2,500 children. Schools were asked to record details of ethnic background along the lines of the categories used in the 1991 census; however, numbers in some of the groups were rather small and eventually the only groups used for an analysis were African Caribbean, Indian, Pakistani and white. The Pakistani children tended to obtain lower levels than the other ethnic groups in all three subjects (English, maths and science), while African Caribbean and Indian children tended to obtain lower levels than white children in English and maths, but not in science. The report concludes, 'A major factor in some of these differences was the fact the home language of many of the children from different ethnic origins was not English'[19].

At both the overall subject level, and the detailed attainment target level, *the group who spoke English at home scored significantly higher* in all three subjects (for both teacher assessment and the SAT).

The focus on levels of fluency is, of course, important; but, while it may explain differences between the ethnic majority and Indian or Pakistani groups, it does not necessarily explain the difference between the Pakistani and Indian samples, nor between the ethnic majority and African Caribbean groups. Unfortunately, the study did not look at ethnic group and social class together.

The Department for Education and Employment (DfEE) analyses of Key Stage 1 data do not use ethnic group. Consequently, LEA analyses are the major source of information at this stage. The Key Stage 1 analyses for 1994 for Wandsworth show all three ethnic minority groups analysed (Pakistani, Indian and 'Black Caribbean') scoring below the average - the performance of Pakistani pupils in English, and black pupils in maths, giving particular cause for concern. Pupils who were fully bilingual achieved slightly better than monolingual English speakers, while those who were not fluent in English scored less well in all subjects[20]. The Year 6 test results for 1994 show that the mean score for the Indian, Pakistani, Bangladeshi and Chinese groups was *below* the average on the Reading Test, but *above* average on the maths test; this seems to reflect the proportion of pupils in the groups (40 - 51 per cent) who were not fully fluent in English. However, the black pupils were the lowest scoring group in both tests: analysis which takes into account the fact that this group was the most economically disadvantaged still shows black pupils to be scoring low.

Results over the three years 1992 - 1994 indicate a widening gap at Year 6 between the average reading and maths score of black pupils and the average for the LEA[21].

To summarise, the overall picture is complex and changing. There is evidence that at the primary phase, in London at least, the performance of African Caribbean and some Asian pupils gives considerable cause for concern. Interestingly, this is not replicated in Birmingham. The good performance of young African Caribbean pupils in Birmingham merits continuing attention.

2.3 ACHIEVEMENT AT THE END OF COMPULSORY EDUCATION

Measuring achievement at 16

Educational qualifications can be vitally important to young people. Studies of the youth labour market suggest that selection processes often present another layer of disadvantage to be faced by black and Asian young people. Young people of ethnic minority background suffer much higher rates of unemployment than similarly qualified whites[22]. Nevertheless, minority pupils with qualifications generally fare better than those without[23]. Although qualifications cannot guarantee access to education or employment they are often a necessary precondition: without qualifications, young people face a restricted range of opportunities. Pupils' examination results at 16 offer a relatively strong and reliable basis for comparison.

The GCSE is a nationally recognised form of assessment that enjoys good professional credibility. Recent years have seen attempts to improve the range and standing of vocational courses and, for some pupils, these offer an important supplement or alternative to GCSE. The GCSE, however, remains the most common, and best understood, form of assessment at the end of compulsory education. For these reasons we have chosen to focus on GCSE results as the principal criterion for measuring achievement at the end of compulsory schooling. The next issue to be resolved is how we count those results. There is no wholly satisfactory measure of examination performance at 16 plus. The three most commonly used measures each reveal something of importance but their interpretation is fraught with difficulties:

(a) *Five or more higher grade (A*-C) passes* [24]

This reflects the historical importance of five separate 'O' level passes as an entry requirement for many 'old' universities. It is the most commonly quoted statistic in the annually published performance tables, but has been criticized for focusing only on the performance of the highest achieving students. Additionally this measure does not distinguish between different subjects. The core subjects (especially English and maths) often carry special weight in attempts to enter further education or the professions: recently published data suggest that Black Caribbean young people may be achieving markedly below the level of their white peers in mathematics and science - but such differences are lost in composite measures of attainment[25].

(b) *One or more GCSE pass grades (A*-G)*

This indicates how many pupils leave compulsory schooling with at least a minimum of formal certification. However, it is not a good basis for general comparison because the range of grades is so broad.

(c) *Exam scores*

An increasingly popular measure of GCSE achievement involves assigning a numerical score to each pass grade achieved (eight points for a grade A*, seven for a grade A, six for a grade B, and so on) and totalling the scores for each individual. This measure is favoured by many because it gives credit to all grades and reflects both the quantity and quality of grades achieved. By calculating the average performance score for certain groups of pupils we can more fairly compare the overall academic achievement of different groups - taking account of the full range of performance, rather than focusing on the extremes. As with the other measures, however, it is necessary to exercise caution. An exam score of 25, for example, is the equivalent of five higher grade passes (all at grade C) or one higher grade pass (at grade B) plus six lower grade passes (three at D, two at E, one at G).

Class, gender and ethnic origin: understanding the interconnections

Ethnic origin is only one of several factors that may be significant in judging achievement. Social class and gender are also important issues that sometimes cut across the influence of ethnicity.

Social class is a deceptively simple term: although most people have some understanding of 'the class system' there is no single scale upon which everyone is agreed. Most research uses a combination of income and perceived differences in status - dividing occupations into discrete and hierarchical groups. Researchers often focus on a split between manual and non-manual workers - even to the extent of using this to approximate 'working' and 'middle' class respectively[26].

> • When information on pupils' social class background is collected, there is usually a direct relationship with academic achievement; the higher the social class, the higher the achievement.

In Nottingham, for example, children from 'professional' backgrounds recently achieved an average exam score more than double the figure for children from 'manual' backgrounds[27]. Unfortunately, data on social class is often absent from research because it is difficult to collect sufficiently detailed information.

The relationship between gender and achievement has recently enjoyed considerable attention. Overall, girls do slightly better than boys in their GCSE examinations, reflecting a pattern that has developed over several years[28]. However, boys achieve more highly at 'A' level and there are still considerable differences in the kinds of subject entered by pupils of either sex[29].

Both social class and gender are important variables when considering pupils' GCSE achievements. Nevertheless, it is exceptional to find studies of achievement by ethnic minority pupils that give full attention to *both* these factors. Table 2.1 summarises the results of a project (the Youth Cohort Study - YCS) that *does* offer this information. Based on

Table 2.1

Average examination scores by social class, ethnic origin and gender (1985)

Ethnic and social class group		Average exam score		Number of
		Male	Female	Cases
African Caribbean				
	Professional	27.1	24.9	12
	Intermediate	21.1	18.1	68
	Manual	14.3	15.6	115
Asian				
	Professional	30.7	27.8	17
	Intermediate	27.2	25.9	95
	Manual	23.3	22.5	189
White				
	Professional	30.4	32.3	2,118
	Intermediate	23.7	25.6	3,903
	Manual	17.6	20.6	5,218

Source: Drew and Gray, 1990, adapted from p. 114, Table 5.

examination results in 1985, it shows the average exam performance scores for pupils arranged by social class (professional, intermediate, manual), ethnic background (African Caribbean, Asian, white) and gender.

> • Social class is strongly associated with achievement regardless of gender and ethnic background: *whatever the pupils' gender or ethnic origin,* those from the higher social class backgrounds do better on average.

This confirms earlier research cited by the Swann Committee, but is more reliable because of the size and nature of the sample used. Unlike almost every other piece of research in this field, Table 2.1 is based on a *nationally representative* sample. It also suggests that the relationship between gender and achievement may not be as simple as predicted - in this case, the pattern of girls out-performing boys was only uniformly true for white pupils: it was not true of Asian pupils in any social class group and only applied to African Caribbean pupils from manual backgrounds.

When presented graphically (Figure 2.1) the differences between ethnic groups become clearer.

Figure 2.1

Average exam scores by ethnic origin, gender and social class (England & Wales, 1985)

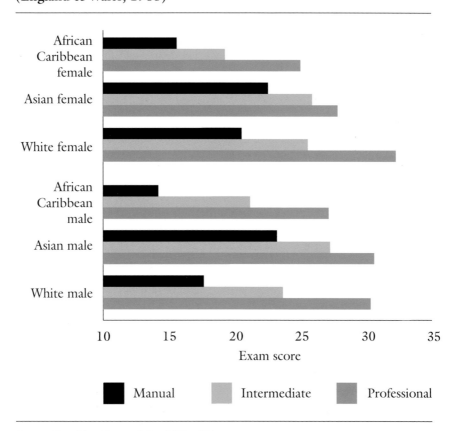

Source: Adapted from Drew and Gray, 1990, p.114

On average, African Caribbean pupils (of both sexes) achieved below the level attained by the other groups. Asian pupils, on the other hand, achieved almost as well as, or better than, whites of the same class and gender.

Overall the average gap between the African Caribbean and white pupils was around five exam points (equivalent to an additional higher grade pass)[30]. These results confirm the general perception of differences in achievement proposed by the Swann report and reproduced in a number of separate studies during the 1980s[31]. These views had been criticised for their failure to take account of social class factors[32], but the Youth Cohort Study (YCS) suggests the general patterns may have been accurately represented. However, the data are not without weaknesses: the sample, although large in total, contains relatively few minority pupils from non-manual backgrounds (see Table 2.1), making generalization difficult.

Furthermore, the ethnic categories are crude. There is no distinction between, for example, pupils of Indian, Pakistani and Bangladeshi backgrounds - they are all counted as 'Asian'. This ignores significant differences in the cultural, political and economic profiles of these groups and prevents analysis of differences in achievement *within* the 'Asian' group. This is important because at the time the YCS data were being analysed, statistics from the Inner London Education Authority (ILEA) showed the single most successful group to be Indian pupils (average exam score 24.5) and the least successful to be Bangladeshis (average score 8.7)[33]. Finally, it is important to remember that the YCS material is old. Although the study was published in 1990, the figures refer to examinations taken in the mid 1980s. Despite these limitations, the YCS results remain exceptional in their ability to address simultaneously issues of class, gender and ethnic background: in this way, Table 2.1 and Figure 2.1 offer a fairly reliable snap-shot of the situation a decade ago. The next task is to establish what has happened in the intervening years.

The 1990s: all change?

Overall levels of GCSE achievement have been improving in recent years. The proportion of pupils gaining five or more higher grade (A*-C) passes has risen from 38.3 per cent in 1992 to 43.3 per cent in 1994, while the proportion gaining five or more pass grades (A*-G) has risen from 82.2 per cent to 85.6 percent[34]. Recent findings from the Youth Cohort Study allow us to trace this trend further back: between the YCS sample in 1988 and the Department for Education (DFE) returns for 1994, the proportion of pupils reaching the high hurdle of five higher passes has increased from around 30 per cent to just over 43 per cent - almost half as many again over six years (see Figure 2.2).

The overall improvements are almost totally the product of changing success rates among pupils in state maintained schools - the independent sector performing at a relatively stable level during the period. The same research indicates that *girls have improved at a faster rate than boys*. However, since 1990, YCS analyses have not addressed ethnic background as a major focus and so recent YCS reports do not tell us whether all ethnic groups share equally in the GCSE improvements. For information on the relative improvements of different ethnic groups we must turn to new data we have gathered from local authorities[35].

Ethnic monitoring is increasingly viewed as 'an integral part of education practice' that may help to identify areas of possible discrimination and inequality[36]. Since 1990, the DFE have expected all LEA maintained and grant maintained schools to collect information on the ethnic background of their pupils. Local authorities, however, are under no obligation to analyse examination results in relation to ethnic origin. Consequently, the resulting pattern of information is rather haphazard; even in LEAs that serve substantial ethnic minority communities, we found that practice varied considerably. Some conduct quite thorough statistical analyses; several either do not collect or choose not to publish information on pupils' ethnic background. Of those LEAs that do analyse exam results by ethnic origin, almost all report some form of improvement over recent years. LEAs differ considerably, however, in the number of years they trace results back, in the ethnic categories they use and in their attempts simultaneously to examine class and gender factors. Consequently we cannot produce any meaningful aggregate tables from across all the LEA returns - instead, we will try to summarize the major findings that emerge from the data.

Figure 2.2

Pupils gaining five or more GCSE higher grade (A*-C) passes (1988-94)

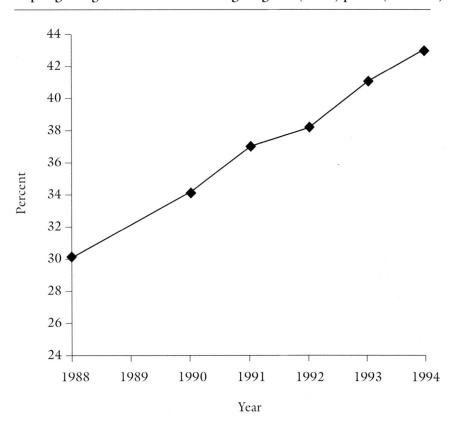

Source: Adapted from DfEE performance tables and Payne, 1995, p.6

Of all English LEAs, the London Borough of Brent serves the largest proportion of ethnic minority pupils[37]. Brent's statistics have several factors to recommend them; they refer to relatively large ethnic minority pupil populations, describe up to a four year period and also examine the importance of pupil gender. As always there are problems - in this case the lack of information on social class background and the adoption of fairly crude ethnic categories (African Caribbean; Asian; white). Data on Brent show an overall increase in the average exam score from 24.8 in 1990 to 33.5 in 1994 - an increase of more than a third over four years, and equivalent to an additional pass at the highest grade. When the material is broken down by ethnicity, it emerges that *pupils in each major ethnic group enjoyed increased success - but not equally so*[38].

Figure 2.3

Pupils gaining five or more GCSE higher grade (A*-C) passes by ethnic origin. Brent, both sexes (1991-93)

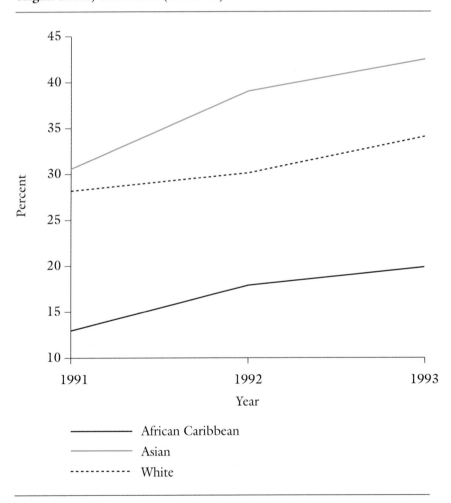

Source: Brent, 1994

In Brent, the most successful group are pupils of 'Asian' ethnic origin; their average exam score rose from 30 to 38 points between 1991 and 1993 (+8 points). This compares with changes from 26.9 to 32.3 (+5.4) for white pupils, and 19.1 to 25.6 (+6.5) for African Caribbeans. Although each ethnic group achieved increased success, therefore, *the gap grew between the highest and lowest achieving groups* ('Asian' and African Caribbean respectively) - a pattern that was true for both sexes. In terms of the proportion gaining five or more higher grade (A-C) passes, a similar picture emerged - summarized in Figure 2.3.

In Brent, girls tend to perform rather better than boys, although ethnic origin continues to be a significant factor. In the latest available statistics, almost one in two Asian and white girls achieved the high hurdle of five or more higher grade passes, but less than one in four African Caribbean girls. More than one in three Asian and one in four white boys achieved five or more higher grades: the equivalent figure for African Caribbean boys was around one in six. However, African Caribbean boys are not necessarily in the worst position: among pupils in Brent leaving school without any pass grades (A-G), white boys stand out as the most likely to be completely unqualified on leaving compulsory education - true for almost one in ten white young men in Brent, around one in 25 African Caribbeans and one in 200 Asians.

It would be easy to read too much significance into results from a single London borough. In particular we should remember that the white population of London is not representative of the social class composition of whites more generally - tending to be skewed more heavily towards people with working class backgrounds[39]. Since Brent data contain no measure of class background, this may have the effect of seeming to depress the relative performance of white pupils.

Although Brent has the largest *proportion* of pupils from ethnic minority backgrounds, Birmingham has the largest minority population in terms of *absolute* size[40]. GCSE results in Birmingham show a steady increase in the proportion of pupils gaining five or more higher grade passes; rising from 18 per cent in 1988 to 30 per cent in 1994 - an improvement of two thirds over a seven year period. However, as in Brent, these gains have not been enjoyed equally by all groups. The 1994 data reveal an increasing gap between the highest achieving group (white pupils) and the lowest achieving group (African Caribbean). Over the three years 1992 to 1994, the proportion of white pupils gaining five or more higher passes rose from 32 per cent to 36 per cent (+4 per cent); the proportion of African Caribbean pupils achieving such success rose initially (from 13 per cent in 1992 to 16 per cent in 1993) but then fell back (14 per cent in 1994). Consequently the overall gap between white and African Caribbean pupils has grown. In 1994 just over one in three whites achieved at least five higher grades; the same was true of around one in seven African Caribbean pupils[41] (see Figure 2.4).

Although LEAs differ considerably in their ethnic and social class compositions, therefore, some general patterns do emerge from the data - not forgetting the wide variety in counting methods and ethnic categories. With these limitations in mind, and confining ourselves to the largest ethnic groups in each authority, the following conclusions can be drawn from the LEA data we have received:

- The general improvement in GCSE achievement has been experienced, to some degree, across almost all LEAs.

- Pupils from many different ethnic backgrounds have achieved improved performances - no groups have been universally exempted. LEA data show improvements by pupils from many different ethnic backgrounds. The scale of the improvements is frequently quite dramatic, although, of course, many statistics are based on relatively small numbers of pupils. In terms of the largest ethnic minority groups, the LEA data include examples of improvement by all (including Indian, Pakistani, Bangladeshi, Black Caribbean, Black African and Chinese). This does not mean, however, that pupils in every category have

Figure 2.4

Pupils gaining five or more GCSE higher grade (A*-C) passes by ethnic origin. Birmingham, both sexes (1992-94)

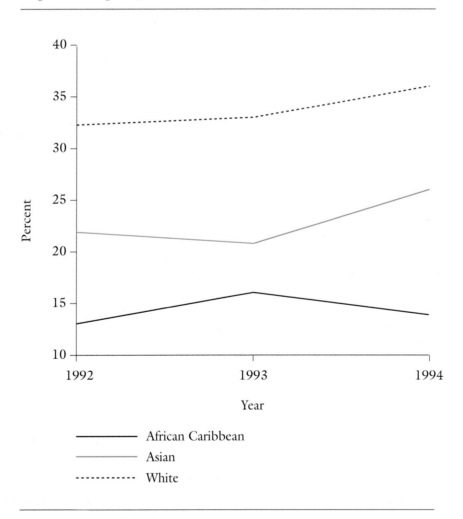

Source: Birmingham Local Education Authority.

always improved (either every year or in every LEA). Indeed, 'black' and/or 'Caribbean' pupils have suffered a fall in average achievements in some areas (see below).

- The gap has widened between the most successful and least successful groups. In general the LEA returns indicate that greater improvements in GCSE results have been made by the ethnic groups that already faired best locally. Despite improvements in the achievements of other groups, therefore, the gap between the different groups has frequently increased.

Achievement by the largest ethnic minority groups

The absence of nationally representative research means that *no definitive conclusions are possible about the relative achievements of each ethnic group*. The best available solution is to pull together the most important trends to emerge from locally based figures (both academic and LEA produced).

South Asian pupils

As we have seen, research conducted in the 1980s tended to show 'Asian' pupils performing, on average, to levels that are as good as, or better than, white pupils. Much of this work was based on London, however, and because of its social class profile we should be careful about generalisations based on the capital. In Birmingham, which has the largest population of South Asian pupils in the country, GCSE results (for 1992 to 1994 inclusive) show 'Asian' pupils performing *less well* on average than their white peers, but significantly better than the African Caribbean group - a pattern that is repeated by both sexes (see Figure 2.4).

The use of the broad category 'Asian' is being increasingly challenged, not least because it ignores important differences in the economic, social and religious profile of different communities. The need to break down this category is demonstrated in recent statistics from Birmingham which, of all English authorities, includes the greatest number of Pakistani pupils and the second largest Indian and Bangladeshi populations[42]. The 1995 GCSE results used a more detailed breakdown of the Asian population for the first time: Indian pupils were found to achieve average results marginally better than their white peers of the same sex. In contrast, Pakistani and Bangladeshi pupils were less likely to achieve five or more higher grades and more likely to leave school without any qualifications[43].

Indian pupils

People of Indian ethnic background make up around 28 per cent of Britain's minority population[44]. In the 1980s, research in inner London suggested that Indian pupils achieved better on average than any other ethnic group, including the white population[45]. More recent results from Brent suggest that Indian pupils may still be out-performing their white peers in London[46]. We have noted, however, that because of its social class profile, the capital's white population may appear relatively poor in comparison with other groups. Certainly evidence from outside London does not support the idea that Indian pupils are universally out-performing their white peers. Although Indian pupils achieve more highly than whites in Birmingham, for example, in Lancashire the average exam score for whites is greater than each of the largest minority groups: in the case of Indian pupils the difference is 4.5 points - roughly equivalent to an additional higher grade pass[47]. There is, therefore, no simple uniform pattern. Published research and the LEA data we have collected support two general conclusions:

- Indian pupils are achieving levels of success consistently in excess of their white counterparts in some (but not all) urban areas.

- among South Asian pupils, those of Indian ethnic origin tend to achieve the highest average results.

In Bradford in 1994, for example, Indian pupils achieved an average exam score more than 10 points higher than the Pakistani and Bangladeshi groups - equivalent to an additional two higher grade (C) passes at GCSE[48]. Clearly this is an area where further research is needed: it would be especially helpful to examine the contribution of social class factors since of all the major ethnic groups, the Indian population has the largest proportion in non-manual occupations[49].

Pakistani pupils

Although the Pakistani community is one of the largest minority groups in the country, information about the particular achievements of Pakistani pupils is sparse. Among English LEAs, Bradford has the highest proportion of Pakistani pupils (around one in five 5-15 year olds)[50]. Bradford's achievement data are mostly analysed using a split between 'Asian' and 'non-Asian' pupils. Since 1991, both groups have achieved increasing rates of exam success, although the Asian group have consistently scored around 4.6 points below the average for non-Asians[51]. These are crude categories, however, and the most recent statistics reveal important differences within both groups. Pakistani pupils achieved an average exam score of 23.3 - better than Bangladeshi pupils (21.1), but below the levels achieved by their peers who were categorized as 'Black' (26.1), White (30.1) and Indian (34.4)[52]. Similarly, in Lancashire (which caters for the third largest group of Pakistani pupils in England), they averaged an exam score of 25.3 in 1993, markedly lower than the score of 34.6 for the white group - a difference almost equivalent to two additional higher grade (C) passes.

In contrast, some London boroughs indicate relatively higher performances by Pakistani pupils. Once again, however, the London statistics must be viewed with caution; the influence of social class is rarely taken into account and the number of pupils involved is usually rather small[53]. It appears that in general, therefore, *on average Pakistani pupils are not achieving as highly as their white peers.*

Bangladeshi pupils

People of Bangladeshi ethnic origin make up the smallest of Britain's main South Asian communities[54] but have been the focus of attention among some educationists. This is partly a reflection of research in the 1980s that suggested Bangladeshi pupils were achieving considerably below the level of other ethnic groups[55]. Additionally, it was known that the Bangladeshi community presented a particular historical and economic profile which meant they might face additional barriers to success. Specifically, they are not as long established as other South Asian groups and are less often fluent in English. In terms of social class, relatively more Bangladeshi people are employed in manual occupations than any of the other major ethnic groups[56].

Figure 2.5

Average exam score by ethnic group. Tower Hamlets, both sexes (1990-94)

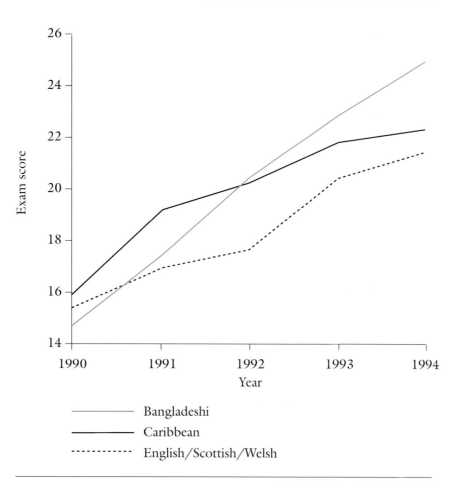

Source: Tower Hamlets, 1994.

The combined influence of these factors can often be seen in the relatively poorer performance of Bangladeshi pupils. The London Borough of Camden, for example, caters for the fifth largest number of Bangladeshi pupils in England. Here just over 30 per cent of Bangladeshi pupils 'were classified by their schools as being at Stages 1 and 2 of English language development (i.e. bilingual pupils new to, or becoming familiar with English), far more than for any other ethnic group'[57]. In this LEA, in comparison with 'Black' and white pupils, Bangladeshis traditionally are entered for fewer exams and achieve lower average exam scores[58]. Yet this pattern is not inevitable.

The London Borough of Tower Hamlets houses almost a quarter of all Bangladeshi children aged 5-15 in England[59]. The borough has made a priority of identifying and targeting the needs of Bangladeshi pupils, especially through the use of Section 11 funds. Recent years have seen improvements in the average exam scores of pupils in each of the borough's major ethnic groups, but the achievements of Bangladeshi pupils are especially dramatic (see Figure 2.5): as a group, Bangladeshi pupils now achieve higher average exam scores than both white and 'Caribbean' pupils in the borough. This is despite experiencing greater levels of economic disadvantage[60]. It would appear, therefore, that Bangladeshi pupils in Tower Hamlets are able to transcend social class relatively more than their white and Caribbean peers; nevertheless, social class continues to be strongly associated with achievement in as much as each group attains below the national average.

In this case, the LEA argues that because poverty is widespread among the Bangladeshi group, other factors - especially language fluency - come to exert greater influence over levels of achievement[61]. Recent statistics confirm a strong relationship between stages of fluency and the achievement of pupils for whom English is a second language (ESL). In Tower Hamlets, ESL pupils are graded according to a four point scale from 1 (beginners) to 4 (fully fluent). Figure 2.6 shows the association between stages of fluency and achievement according to three common measures. Significantly, by Stage 3, bilingual pupils are achieving better averages than English-only speakers. This demonstrates the importance of language support beyond the most basic levels of need: continued support to help pupils become reasonably fluent in English can be directly reflected in GCSE results.

The results from Tower Hamlets are especially significant because they illustrate the complexity of achievement. Here Bangladeshi pupils, the group most usually associated with high levels of disadvantage and low average achievements, have become the most successful ethnic group in the LEA - despite continued economic disadvantages. The findings warn against over-simplifying the achievements of pupils in any ethnic group.

African and Caribbean pupils

The issue of 'black under-achievement' has been complicated by the problems of categorizing different ethnic groups within the broadly defined 'black' group. Recent practice has moved away from subsuming *all* ethnic minority groups under the heading 'black', not least because most people of ethnic minority origin do not use that term to describe themselves and because it can disadvantage South Asian groups (who are often forgotten when talk turns to 'black' issues)[62]. Additionally, the use of the term 'black' may

Figure 2.6

Achievement and stages of English language fluency, Tower Hamlets (1994)

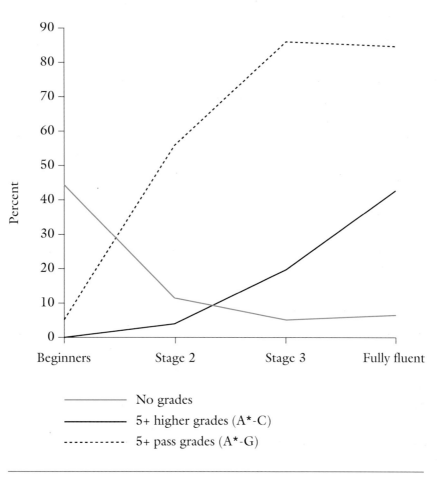

Source: Tower Hamlets, 1994.

obscure significant differences in experience and achievement between pupils with family origins in the Caribbean and those of African ethnic background. The 1991 census indicates that, in comparison to the 'Black African' group, people of Caribbean ethnic origin tended to be less well qualified and to work more often in manual occupations[63]. This is a complex and politically charged area - the term 'African Caribbean', for example, is used by many people to symbolise a shared ethnic heritage and/or position within the British social/economic structure - and yet the census invited people to use *separate* 'Black African' and 'Black Caribbean' labels. The situation is further complicated by the range of terms used by different pieces of research - including 'West Indian', 'Afro-Caribbean' and 'Black British'. In reviewing previous research we are limited by other researchers' categories - nevertheless an awareness of these practical and political problems is essential.

A review of research on minority achievement between the 1970s and 1980s identified a relatively stable picture of African Caribbean pupils achieving less well than peers of the same sex and social class background[64]. We have already described more recent research, mostly at LEA level, that shows this is not a universal pattern. In Tower Hamlets, for example, 'Caribbean' pupils consistently achieve a higher average exam score than their white peers - though recently the gap has narrowed considerably (see Figure 2.5). In Brent, however, African Caribbean pupils have been consistently less successful than the other major ethnic groups (see Figure 2.3). A similar pattern emerges in Birmingham - which has the largest population of black pupils in England. Here, African Caribbean pupils consistently emerge with lower average attainments than their peers of 'Asian' and 'White' ethnic backgrounds[65]. Two broad conclusions immediately suggest themselves:

- The situation is too varied for simple talk of 'black under-achievement'.

- Nevertheless, recent research tends to show African Caribbean pupils as relatively less successful than their 'Asian' and white peers.

The London borough of Lambeth provides an interesting example. In comparison with other English LEAs, the borough has the largest number of Black African pupils aged 5-15 and the second largest number of Afro-Caribbean pupils[66]. In the latest results African pupils achieved an average exam score almost identical to white pupils, whereas the Caribbean group scored around 3 points lower on average (see Table 2.2). The pattern changes significantly, however, when gender is taken into account. As we would predict, based on national returns, girls achieve more highly on average than boys - this is true for each of the three ethnic groups in the table. Yet the table shows very small differences between the performance of girls of different ethnic backgrounds: the ethnic differences are more pronounced in the performance of boys - where Caribbean young men achieved the equivalent of a higher grade pass less than the other groups. Clearly the situation is complex but again two broad conclusions are suggested:

- *Pupils of 'Black African' background often achieve relatively higher results than their peers of 'Black Caribbean' origin - where statistics allow distinctions to be made. It seems likely that both social class and gender play a part in this, but further research is required.*

- *On average, Caribbean young men in particular appear to be achieving considerably below their potential.*

Table 2.2
Average examination scores by ethnic origin and gender. Lambeth (1993)

Ethnic group	Average exam score		Mean	(% of age group)
	Male (N)	Female (N)		
African	21.9 (50)	26.5 (48)	24.2	(9.9%)
Caribbean	15.1 (110)	26.6 (124)	21.2	(23.5%)
Eng, Scot, Welsh	19.8 (88)	27.5 (140)	24.5	(22.9%)

Source: Lambeth, 1994, adapted from appendix F.

Several prominent studies have, in the past, based their conclusions solely on one LEA: there are dangers in such an approach and this review has sought to pull together results from several different studies (sampling different regions and time periods). Despite differences in methods and definitions, *the relatively lower exam achievements of Caribbean pupils, especially boys, is a common feature in most of the academic and LEA research publications.* Two further points should be noted. First, in some cases neither African nor Caribbean pupils have increased their achievements as much as Asian and white groups - scores have actually fallen in some areas. In Camden, for example, the most recent figures indicate a decrease in the performance of 'Black' pupils (see Table 2.3). Similarly, in Southwark pupils categorized as 'Caribbean' achieved less well in the most recent statistics[67]. Consequently, we can reasonably conclude that:

- *on average, black pupils have not shared equally in the increasing rates of educational achievement.*

A second important conclusion arises from this:

- *black pupils generally may be falling further behind the average achievements of the majority of their peers.*

This trend is especially pronounced where the achievements of black pupils have fallen while overall averages have risen. In one LEA between 1993 and 1994, for example, the gap between the average performance of black pupils and the LEA as a whole increased almost equivalent to an additional higher grade pass. At the same time, there was also an increase in the discrepancy between the proportion of pupils gaining five or more higher passes: achieved by one in three pupils in the LEA as a whole, but only one in five black pupils (see Table 2.3).

Table 2.3
Relative achievement of black pupils compared with LEA averages.
Camden (1993 and 1994)

| | Average exam score | | | Percentage with 5+grades A*-C | | |
	1993	1994	(+/-)	1993	1994	(+/-)
Black	25.5	23.8	(-1.7)	23.5%	20.0%	(-3.5%)
All pupils	27.2	30.1	(+2.9)	32.2%	36.6%	(+4.4%)
Black/LEA gap	1.7	6.3	(+4.6)	8.7%	16.6%	(+7.9%)

Source: Camden, 1995, adapted from table 3.

As with the Bangladeshi group, this pattern is not inevitable. One LEA, for example, provided details of a special project (funded using Section 11 resources) that uses a targeted programme of support and tuition: the project has produced real improvements in the average achievements of Caribbean pupils (see Table 2.4). The project includes three secondary schools at present (so the numbers involved are small) and, of course, the improvements only refer to a single year. Nevertheless, the gains are significant and confirm that differences in rates of achievement are not in any way fixed.

Table 2.4

Raising the GCSE achievements of Caribbean pupils. Three schools, Lambeth (1992-1993)

	5+ A-C grades		1+ A-C grades		5+ A-G grades		No A-G grade	
	1992	1993	1992	1993	1992	1993	1992	1993
Caribbean pupils in three targetted secondary schools	11.1	15.3	46.9	60.0	79.0	81.2	24.7	4.7

Source: London Borough of Lambeth, *Raising Achievement Project*, annual report to Home Office 1993/94, adapted from appendices 3 and 4.

Achievement by diverse ethnic groups

Most research on race and ethnicity concentrates on the largest of the ethnic minority communities - concerning people of Indian, Afro-Caribbean, Pakistani, African and Bangladeshi ethnic origins respectively. Along with those of Chinese ethnic background, these groups account for more than eight out of ten of Britain's ethnic minority population. The number of pupils from other ethnic minority backgrounds is not insignificant; because of their uneven geographical location, however, it is not possible to arrive at any firm conclusions about their overall levels of achievement. The Chinese group is a case in point. Although they make up more than five per cent of Britain's minority population, people of Chinese ethnic origin are rarely concentrated in significant numbers in any single LEA[68]. Several of the returns we have examined indicate Chinese pupils achieving significantly above LEA averages. It is difficult to have confidence in these results as wider indicators of educational success, however, because they are often based on very small numbers. Lambeth, for example, has the second largest population of Chinese pupils (aged 5-15), and yet the 1994 exam results were based on just 25 young people[69].

NOTES TO SECTION 2

1 Gipps and Murphy (1994, p. 114-15).

2 Coleman (1968); see also Halsey, Heath and Ridge (1980).

3 Kamin (1974), Gould (1981) and Gipps and Murphy (1994) offer critical reviews of the use and misuse of IQ testing. Herrnstein and Murray (1994) is the most prominent recent example of such IQism: for critiques see Drew, Fosam and Gillborn (1995) and Richardson (1994).

4 Rampton (1981, p.10, original emphasis). This conclusion was subsequently echoed by the full report (Swann, 1985, p. 63).

5 See Troyna (1984).

6 Smith and Tomlinson (1989, Table 16.9, pp. 261-2).

7 See, for example, Eggleston, Dunn and Anjali (1986, pp. 74-9) and Smith and Tomlinson (1989, p. 106).

8 Mortimore et al (1988).

9 See section 4 later in this review.

10 Sammons (1994).

11 Tizard et al (1988).

12 Plewis (1991).

13 Plewis and Veltman (1994).

14 *Times Educational Supplement*, 9 December 1994, p. 9.

15 Birmingham LEA statistics for GCSE results in 1992-1994 consistently show African Caribbean pupils performing less well on average than their 'Asian' and white peers. The pattern is true for both sexes.

16 *Times Educational Supplement*, 9 December 1994, p. 9.

17 Birmingham City Council (1994).

18 Wandsworth (1995).

19 ENCA (1992, p. 101).

20 Wandsworth (1994a).

21 Wandsworth (1994b).

22 Runnymede Trust (1995a, p. 12).

23 See, for example, Brown (1992), Clough and Drew (1985), Drew (1995).

24 GCSE results are graded: A*, A, B, C, D, E, F, G, U (unclassified). Grades C and above are considered to be 'higher grade' passes, roughly equivalent to pass grades in the old General Certificate of Education (GCE) 'O' level examinations.

25 In one metropolitan authority, in 1994, 35.2 per cent of white pupils gained A*-C grades in mathematics, compared to 7 per cent of Black Caribbeans (*Times Educational Supplement*, 26 April 1996, TES 2, p. 3).

26 Craft and Craft (1983).

27 In 1993 children from 'professional' backgrounds scored an average of 43.9 exam points; 'clerical' scored 33.1 and 'manual' 20.8 (Farnsworth, Everett and Jesson, 1994, p. 12).

28 See, for example, Sammons (1994) and Thomas, Pan and Goldstein (1994).

29 For more detail on the processes underlying subject choice and gender differences see Delamont (1990), Gillborn (1990), Measor and Sikes (1992) and Riddell (1992).

30 Drew and Gray (1991, p. 163).

31 In addition to their own data from the YCS, for example, Drew and Gray (1991) summarise the results of six separate studies of ethnic origin and achievement: Maughan and Rutter (1986), Mabey (1986), the Rampton report (1981), the Swann report (1985), Eggleston et al (1986) and Kysel (1988). Based on material gathered in the period 1972 to 1985 these studies tend to produce a stable picture of the relative achievements of white, Asian and African Caribbean pupils.

32 Troyna (1984).

33 Kysel (1988).

34 Source, Department for Education and Employment.

35 The appendix to this report contains details of the LEAs we approached.

36 Commission for Racial Equality (1992a, p. 7).

37 The Small Area Statistics (SAS) component of the 1991 census indicates that white young people account for around 38 per cent of 5-15 year olds in Brent.

38 Brent publish overall data from 1990, but ethnic breakdowns from 1991 onwards (Brent, 1994).

39 Nuttall, Goldstein, Prosser and Rasbash (1989, p. 774).

40 In 1991 around 206,800 people of ethnic minority origin lived in Birmingham - almost seven per cent of the entire minority population of the country (Runnymede Trust, 1994, p. 14-15).

41 We are grateful to Pratap Deshpande and John Hill for compiling these data especially for this review.

42 1991 census, small area statistics, pupils aged 5-15. See Birmingham (1995).

43 In 1995, 35.7 per cent of white pupils (boys and girls) achieved five or more higher grade GCSE passes; less than the 39.4 per cent of Indian pupils, but more than Bangladeshis (28.7 per cent), Pakistanis (20.9 per cent) and African Caribbeans (17.6 per cent). For those achieving no graded results the figures were Indian 5.9 per cent; white 10.4 per cent; Pakistani 13 per cent; African Caribbean 13.6 per cent; Bangladeshi 17.6 per cent. Source, Birmingham LEA (personal communication).

44 1991 census. See also Runnymede Trust (1994, p. 13).

45 Kysel (1988).

46 Brent schools cater for the fourth largest group of Indian pupils in the country. As we have seen, 'Asian' pupils in Brent (most of whom are Indian) achieve higher results on average than either their white or African Caribbean peers (Brent, 1994).

47 In Lancashire, Indian pupils scored 30.1 on average, compared with 34.6 by whites (Thomas and Mortimore, 1994, p. 15).

48 Bradford Education Department (1994, p. 23).

49 In a ten per cent sample of the 1991 census, almost 6 out of ten (58.4 per cent) of the Indian population were categorized as in non-manual occupations: this compares with 56.5 per cent of whites, 46.7 per cent of Pakistanis and 36.8 per cent of Bangladeshis. Source: Runnymede Trust (1994, p. 26).

50 1991 census, small areas statistics.

51 Bradford Education Department (1994, p. 9).

52 Bradford Education Department (personal communication).

53 In 1993 exams in one borough , 38.6 per cent of GCSE grades attained by Pakistani pupils were in the A-C range; better than most other groups - including African (33.7%), Bangladeshi (33.2%), 'Caribbean' (21.9%) and 'English, Scots, Welsh' (27.6%). Unfortunately, the figures relate to just 54 entries, between seven Pakistani pupils (Southwark, 1994, p. 36).

54 In 1991, people of Bangladeshi ethnic origin accounted for 0.3 per cent of the total population; that is 5.4 per cent of the ethnic minority population.

55 Kysel (1988), ILEA (1990) and Tomlinson (1992).

56 According to the 1991 census, 58.7 per cent of Bangladeshis worked in manual occupations. The next highest proportion was 49.7 per cent (Pakistani). The figure for whites was 41.8 per cent (Runnymede Trust, 1994, p. 26).

57 Camden (1995, para. 3.4).

58 In 1994 , the average exam scores were: Bangladeshi 22.0, Black 23.8, ESW (white) 30.5 - a gap between white and Bangladeshi of 8.5, equivalent to an additional higher pass at grade A*, or two extra passes at grade D.

59 12,394 of the 50,931 Bangladeshis aged 5-15: source, self assessed ethnic identification in the Small Area Statistics component of the 1991 census.

60 In 1994, 86 per cent of Bangladeshi pupils were eligible for free school meals, compared to 47 per cent of Caribbean and 39 per cent of white pupils (Tower Hamlets, 1994, p. 11).

61 Tower Hamlets (1994, p. 11).

62 The Commission for Racial Equality ceased to recommend classifying Asians as 'black' in the late 1980s (CRE, 1988a) - a decision echoed in the 1991 census. See also Modood (1992).

63 In terms of people with relatively high educational qualifications (diploma and above), the data for those aged 18 and over were: African, male 31 per cent, female 22 per cent. Caribbean, male 6 per cent, female 12 per cent (Drew and Fosam, 1994, p. 6 and Figure 2). In terms of social class, the proportions occupied in non-manual and manual occupations respectively were African 57.1 per cent and 38 per cent, Afro-Caribbean 52 per cent and 48 per cent (Runnymede Trust, 1994, p. 26).

64 Drew and Gray (1991).

65 Birmingham's GCSE results are reported using the category 'African Caribbean'. In fact, the LEA serves relatively few pupils from 'Black African' backgrounds: less than half of one per cent of the population aged 5-15. In contrast, more than 10,000 pupils were categorized as 'Black Caribbean' in the census: around seven per cent of the Birmingham population aged 5-15. GCSE results for the years 1992 to 1994 inclusive show white pupils achieving the highest average performances, followed by those of 'Asian' ethnic origin. Data for 1995 show African Caribbean boys performing particularly badly: 33.5 per cent of white males achieved five or more higher grade passes compared with 12.8 per cent of African Caribbean males. For females the figures were white 38 per cent; African Caribbean 22.9 per cent. Source, Birmingham LEA (personal communication).

66 1991 census, small area statistics. In using census material here we have combined the categories 'Caribbean' and 'Black other' into the single group, 'Afro-Caribbean'. See Ballard and Kalra (1994) and Runnymede Trust (1994, p. 10).

67 In Southwark, Caribbean pupils achieved A-C grades in 25.9 per cent of examinations in 1992, but this fell to 21.9 per cent in 1993 (Southwark, 1994, p. 36).

68 1991 Census data; see Runnymede Trust (1994, p. 12).

69 Lambeth (1994, appendix F).

3 Educational Progress and School Effectiveness

The last decade has seen remarkable advances in the scope and sophistication of educational research. Advances in research methods, however, do not guarantee subsequent improvements in the understanding, awareness and practice of the major users of research. New words and phrases have entered the language of education (value added; school effectiveness) but their wider impact on teaching and learning is uncertain. There is a good deal of confusion about the meaning of these ideas. For this reason, this section begins by exploring some of the basic techniques and assumptions underlying research on educational progress and school effectiveness; it then turns to research on the relative progress made by different ethnic groups and, finally, considers the wider field of school effectiveness and 'value added' approaches.

3.1 CLARIFYING THE CONCEPTS

Progress

In its most basic sense, 'progress' refers to the difference in a pupil's performance between two time points, say between assessments made at transfer from primary to secondary school and their final performance in GCSE examinations. One point is vital:

- 'progress' and 'achievement' are not the same.

Normally we would expect those who make greatest progress also to achieve the highest results; however, if their starting points are different, greater progress may not equate to greater achievement. Take, for example, the two groups of pupils represented in Figure 3.1.

Figure 3.1

Differences in progress are not the same as differences in achievement

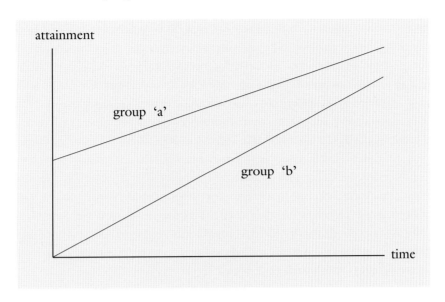

At the start, group 'a' has attained a higher average than group 'b'. Over the period represented in the illustration, both groups make progress: the lines between the start and end points slope upward. At the end of the period, in comparison with their *prior attainment*, group 'b' has made the most progress (their line has the steepest slope). However, group 'a' still achieves at a higher level. In this way, it is possible that despite making greater *progress*, a group may not *achieve* as highly as another.

Multilevel modelling

> 'the multilevel approach tells us how well a school is doing relative to the average and other schools'[1]

Multilevel modelling is a statistical technique that attempts to control for the various different influences which might affect pupils' educational performance. In theory, the approach compares the performance of *similar pupils* (in terms of background characteristics and prior attainments) *in different schools* - producing a measure of the relative 'effectiveness' of individual schools. Advocates of multilevel approaches argue that, in comparison with performance tables based on raw examination results, the technique more accurately represents the work of schools because differences in the prior attainment and social background of the pupil intake are taken into account. However, in order to succeed, the approach requires detailed information on individual pupils; such as a measure of prior attainment, social class background, gender and the identity of the school(s) they have attended. Additionally, the interpretation of the statistical findings is open to confusion and dispute[2].

School effectiveness and 'value added' calculations

For general purposes, an effective school can be thought of as 'one in which pupils progress further than might be expected from consideration of its intake'[3]. Unfortunately, talk of school effectiveness now ranges from the specific (based on large samples analysed through multilevel modelling) to the general (with individual observers and practitioners making claims for 'effectiveness' based on raw data and/or intuitive judgements).This problem is especially acute in discussions about the 'value added' by schools. Some use 'value added' as a convenient short-hand for school effectiveness research[4]; others use the phrase to refer to calculations of progress based simply on comparisons between raw results at different points in time. The resulting confusion is captured in the discussions about including a 'value added' component in the DfEE's school performance tables. The Dearing Report, for example, recommended that value added measures be explored as a potentially useful indicator of school performance, but that exploratory work should 'concentrate ... on the development of measures based on *raw* data'[5]. The resulting advice from the School Curriculum and Assessment Authority (SCAA) rejected the general applicability of multilevel modelling despite accepting that it is 'an appropriate way to separate out the degree to which schools affect the progress which their pupils make'[6].

Amid all the technical arguments there are also wider conceptual issues: 'while all reviews assume that effective schools can be differentiated from ineffective ones, there is no consensus yet on just what constitutes an effective school'[7]. It has also been argued that, despite its apparent complexity, school effectiveness research risks over-simplification; reducing education to a series of relatively simple input and output measures. Lawrence Angus has argued that this carries important consequences for how schools, pupils and local communities are thought of:

> Family background, social class, any notion of context, are typically regarded as 'noise' - as 'outside' background factors which must be controlled for and then stripped away so that the researcher can concentrate on the important domain of school factors ... sexism, racism, and any of the other social and educational disadvantages and conflicts that surround and pervade schooling ... may be remotely acknowledged, but they are sanitised in school effectiveness research, reduced to distant 'home background' and regarded merely as quality of input[8].

It might also be argued that multilevel modelling - by controlling for the *separate* influence of different factors - loses sight of the complex *interconnecting* processes that may deny some pupils equal opportunities to succeed. For example, calculations of the progress made by different ethnic groups sometimes control for pupils' social class background and their placement in certain 'ability bands' within a school. Both these factors have been found to be associated with rates of progress and achievement[9]. There is evidence that certain minority pupils (such as those of African Caribbean ethnic origin) are over-represented in lower income groups and in the lower bands in schools. When statistical work looks at these factors separately any cumulative effects are hidden. This is, of course, part of the reason that mult-ilevel models are so popular - because they disentangle multiple factors. It might be argued, however, that by losing sight of the interconnections and cumulative weight of certain factors, such an approach fails to represent the real world of education as it is experienced by many pupils. In school effectiveness research, the progress of African Caribbean pupils will be judged against other ethnic groups *after* taking account of social class, low income and academic band - any extra hurdles they face because of differences in income or placement in low bands will be examined as a feature of social class or banding, not ethnic group.

The issues are complex and raise vital questions about what research can and cannot tell us. There is no simple solution to these dilemmas, but they should be kept in mind when considering statistical work of this kind.

3.2 DIFFERENCES IN EDUCATIONAL PROGRESS

Progress in primary and secondary schools

In a previous section, we discussed the *School Matters* research on junior school pupils in inner London[10]. A follow-up study, by Pam Sammons, gathered information on the pupils' subsequent GCSE achievements, allowing an exploration of changes in rates of progress over a *nine year period* - an exceptional timespan for such research[11]. The project also gained from the very detailed background information that was available on pupils, including separate measures for social class and low income. However, the sample size was depleted by several factors until the secondary sample was less than half the original size (under 1,000 pupils).

This is significant because, like most research in this field, pupils who left secondary education before their examinations - or who were not entered for any GCSEs - could not be included[12]. Since certain minority groups are frequently over-represented in non-examination groups, their absence from the sample may have the effect of making the minority performance levels seem artificially high[13]. Despite these limitations, the research remains significant because it offers a glimpse (albeit an imperfect one) of the importance of various factors over a nine year period that includes both junior and secondary education.

Sammons' work highlights the continued, and increasing, significance of socio-economic factors. As the pupils moved through their education *the influence of low social class background and low family income became more pronounced - a pattern true of both junior and secondary school*[14]. In contrast, after taking account of social class differences, *whereas certain differences between ethnic groups had increased during the junior years, this trend was reversed in secondary school:*

> [in the junior school years] the gap in reading attainment between working class children, those on low incomes, those lacking fluency in English and those of Caribbean backgrounds *increased* over time...[15]

> By the end of compulsory schooling students of Asian backgrounds ... performed significantly *better* than their English, Scots, Welsh and Irish (ESWI) peers, and the Caribbean group's performance was not significantly different[16]

Sammons offers three 'possible explanations' for this pattern, none of which are mutually exclusive.

First, the improvements may reflect the type of assessment used, with GCSE examinations providing a more accurate picture of pupil performance than earlier teacher assessments.

Second, she suggests that minority pupils may have become more motivated during the secondary years, possibly as a result of equal opportunities initiatives or in response to the threat of unemployment in an increasingly competitive youth labour market.

Third, Sammons notes the apparently most obvious possibility, that there has been a 'real' improvement in the relative performance of minority pupils during the secondary years[17].

These suggestions retain the necessary degree of caution about the significance of the results - especially in view of the nature and size of the pupil sample. Nevertheless, the study is an important contribution. Two findings are especially noteworthy:

- *Pupils' performance can vary over time.* Both junior and secondary schools can contribute to pupil performance. *Patterns established in the early years are not fixed.*

- *There is a significant and increasing gap between the performance of pupils from different social class backgrounds.*

Because unemployment is not spread uniformly across society, this finding may have a particular significance for some ethnic minority pupils. In London, black men aged between 16 and 24 are more than three times more likely to be unemployed than whites in the same age group[18]. Nationally, young men of South Asian ethnic background are also more likely to be unemployed than their white counterparts[19]. Although the statistical techniques highlight this as an issue of socio-economic background, its effects may be disproportionately felt among black and Asian young people.

Sammons' findings are broadly supported by other researchers, although many of the problems she encountered are also replicated elsewhere.

Focusing on secondary schools

Prior to the late 1980s, relatively few studies in this field gave ethnic origin any serious attention. Early projects suggested that ethnic minority pupils (especially those of 'Asian' background) made progress that was generally as good as, or better than, their white peers[20]. A critical review of this material, however, pointed to the limited nature of the samples (mostly based on inner London) and cast doubt on the validity of the prior attainment measures used - the accuracy of prior attainment scores is, of course, crucial to calculations of relative progress[21].

Much of the research in London schools uses pupils' allocation to a 'Verbal Reasoning' (VR) band as a measure of their earlier attainment. VR band allocation is decided by teachers' assessments: research on teacher assessments suggests that, on average, minority pupils may be placed in lower groups than suggested by their 'ability' as measured in more formal tests[22]. For African Caribbean pupils this might reflect some teachers' view of them as a disciplinary challenge, or as less highly motivated. For 'Asian' pupils language problems may be misidentified as learning difficulties[23]. Consequently, the apparently greater progress of minority pupils during their secondary schooling may simply reflect teachers' inaccurately low assessments on transfer.

The publication of *'The School Effect'*, in 1989, generated enormous interest in the question of school effectiveness[24]. The book reports a longitudinal study (that is, over a period of time) of pupils in 18 multi-ethnic comprehensive schools and is especially significant for the central role given to questions of ethnic origin. Overall, the authors found that *white pupils attained the best average examination achievements, but minority pupils narrowed the gap during their secondary education, making relatively better progress*[25].

'The School Effect' research has the advantage of sampling schools from diverse geographical locations (including schools in the Midlands and the North of England, as well as London). A major weakness, however, is its 'purposive' sampling design which deliberately sought 'to ensure ... that some of the selected schools were ones thought to be successful, and others less so'[26]. The sample was designed to maximize differences between schools and was, therefore, neither random nor representative. Nevertheless, some support for its findings is offered by more recent research.

An analysis of the 1993 GCSE results in Lancashire also reveals a contrasting picture between absolute achievement and rates of progress. Here too, 'the raw GCSE results indicate that non-White pupils attain lower results on average', but the multilevel analysis shows *some* minority groups made better progress than the white group. The differences were positive and significant for pupils of Indian, Pakistani, Bangladeshi and Chinese backgrounds. However, no significant differences were found between the rates of progress for Black African, Black Caribbean and white pupils[27].

These results are strikingly similar to the findings of a study in seven LEAs - six in London - supported by the Association of Metropolitan Authorities (AMA). To date, three years' results have been analysed (1990; 1991; 1992). There have been changes to the ethnic categories used during the research and so direct comparisons over the three year period 'should be made with caution'. The study indicates 'that only the "Black Caribbean" and "Black Other" groups scored lower than the "White" group, and not significantly so. In contrast, other groups [Black African, Indian, Pakistani, Bangladeshi, Chinese] obtained significantly higher scores'[28]. The authors suggest 'one possible explanation' for the greater progress of some minority groups is that bilingual learners 'may start school as low attainers (in verbal reasoning) but make substantial progress in language skills while attending secondary school'[29].

In general, therefore, most research on the relative *progress* of minority pupils suggests a similar pattern:

- *At the end of junior school, ethnic minority pupils' attainments often lag behind those of white pupils. There is some evidence that the gaps widen during the junior years.*

- *In secondary schools, however, 'Asian' pupils (Indian, Pakistani, Bangladeshi) and those of Chinese ethnic origin tend to make rather better progress than their white peers.*

- *Differences between the progress of the white group and black (African and Caribbean) pupils are generally smaller and less consistent.*

- *Despite making greater progress than their white peers, these same studies generally show minority pupils (except in parts of London) leaving school with worse average achievements in their final examinations.*

Hence, there is no contradiction between the findings in the previous section (that in many areas ethnic minority pupils achieve less highly than their white peers) and multilevel research indicating relatively greater progress by some minority groups. Although some minority pupils are narrowing the gap, during their secondary schooling, they are not closing it entirely.

3.3 RESEARCH ON SCHOOL EFFECTIVENESS AND 'VALUE ADDED'

School effectiveness research enjoys a prominent position in contemporary debates about educational provision and policy: the slogan *'schools make a difference'* has captured the popular imagination. For some, it signals a welcome break from the pessimism of earlier research which seemed to suggest schools could do little to improve achievement in the face of massive inequalities in society at large[30]. For others, the work offers the promise of improving performance in a context of increasingly scarce resources and heightened pressure to deliver better raw examination results. As we have noted, however, there is considerable confusion about school effectiveness research. In this part of the review we want briefly to consider the central questions so far as they tell us anything about the performance of ethnic minority pupils.

The size of school effects

To date, one of the most thorough studies of school effectiveness is the analysis of results in seven LEAs conducted for the AMA. A recent report examines 87 secondary schools and controls for prior attainment, ethnic origin, gender and eligibility for free school meals (as a proxy for social class). The researchers found that overall '12 per cent of the variation in pupils' total examination scores was attributable to schools once the pupil background factors had been taken into account'[31]. However, some schools were found to exert greater influence than others. Indeed, *pupils in just under half the schools were performing around the anticipated levels:* 'Thus 22 schools [out of 87] are significantly better and 28 schools are significantly worse than expected.'[32]. This is an important finding that helps put school effectiveness research into a more balanced perspective.

> • *The largest proportion of schools are performing close to their predicted level: neither significantly better nor worse.*

However, the notion of *overall* effectiveness has itself been questioned. There is growing evidence that separate subject departments, in the same secondary school, can attain rather different levels of value added. Recent analysis of two year's GCSE results, in 94 schools in 1991 and 69 in 1990, suggests that the variation between departmental effectiveness is often greater than the differences between schools' overall levels of effectiveness. In many schools (around a third of the 1991 sample), the researchers found 'substantial departmental differences in terms of effectiveness and these may be masked by a reliance on a single measure of total GCSE score'[33]. According to Harvey Goldstein and his colleagues:

It is clear that there is no single dimension along which schools differ ... It is also clear that the uncertainty attached to individual school estimates, at least based upon a single year's data, is such that fine distinctions and detailed rank orderings are statistically invalid. This has important implications for published 'league tables' whether or not these are adjusted for intake achievement and whether or not multilevel modelling has been used[34].

School effectiveness research is now revealing details of effectiveness that show variability over time and go beyond a simple 'overall' score. For the purposes of this review, however, there is an additional question of an even more pressing nature: *for which pupils are schools effective?*

Effective for whom? The question of differential effectiveness

We have already suggested that some groups have not shared equally in the overall improvement in average GCSE examination performance. The parallel question for school effectiveness research is *do all pupils share in the benefit of an 'effective' school?* Existing research suggests that schools are more effective for certain groups; this is known as 'differential effectiveness'.

Most research on differential effectiveness focuses on the progress of pupils in different 'ability' grades. Recent analyses for the Association of Metropolitan Authorities, for example, show that 'some schools which obtain higher than average results for the most able pupils ... may obtain lower than average results for the least able pupils'[35]. Relatively few projects have investigated whether schools are differentially effective for different ethnic groups. Analysis of the '*School Matters*' data on London primaries found no evidence of significant differential effectiveness for specific ethnic groups[36]. In contrast, work on secondary schools has produced evidence of this, but there is disagreement about the size and significance of the differences.

'*The School Effect*' claimed evidence of differential effectiveness but gave no precise details (such as the size of the differences or the groups concerned); the authors viewed the differences as relatively unimportant and not worthy of further examination[37]. In contrast, research on a much larger sample, over a three year period (drawn from inner London)[38], suggests that differential effectiveness is an important part of the wider picture: 'amongst Pakistani pupils the differences could amount to as much as two O-level passes'[39]. Once again, full details were not reported in the original study, but the authors clearly thought the differences important. Indeed, they highlighted the differences between their own results and those of '*The School Effect*', concluding that 'the concept of overall effectiveness is not useful'[40].

> 'To attempt to summarize school differences, even after adjusting for intake, sex and ethnic background of the students and fixed characteristics of the schools, in a single quantity is misleading[41].'

In conclusion, therefore, two points seem pertinent:

- *There is evidence that some secondary schools are more effective for certain ethnic groups; not all pupils benefit equally from attending apparently 'effective' schools.*

- There is an urgent need for further research on this question.

The issue of schools' differential impact on minority pupils has received little attention. This is a vital area, especially if statistical research can be allied to more sensitive and detailed qualitative (school-based) studies which might help us understand what makes certain schools more effective for particular ethnic groups.

The question of compositional (contextual) effects

A further question concerns the existence of 'compositional' or 'contextual' effects: that is, whether 'the composition of a school's intake can have a substantial effect on pupils' outcome over and above the effects associated with pupils' individual ability and social class'[42]. It has been argued, for example, that pupils of average ability might benefit from attending a school where a large proportion of pupils are of high ability. Alternatively, a school with many less able pupils might depress the performance of more able pupils. This effect could work through a variety of mechanisms; including teacher expectations, peer pressure, parental/community expectations and the ability of the school to recruit and retain experienced teachers[43].

Researchers have found some evidence of compositional effects in secondary (but not primary) schools linked to levels of attainment and social class background. Here pupils of 'average ability' in schools with a relatively high concentration of 'high ability' pupils tended to score 'more highly than comparable students in schools where the majority of pupils were of low ability'[44]. Similarly, negative effects have been reported 'related to the concentration of students eligible for free school meals'[45].

Few studies have considered the possibility of compositional effects related to the ethnic make-up of school populations. To date there is no reliable evidence that the balance of particular ethnic groups in a school has an independent effect on pupils' progress[46]. *'The School Effect'*, for example, concluded:

> 'if balance is a factor influencing progress it is the balance of attainment that is important, rather than the ethnic balance'[47].

It is possible, therefore, that *compositional effects may be restricted to the influence of levels of attainment and social class background within secondary schools.* However, existing research is insufficient for any certain conclusions to be drawn.

NOTES TO SECTION 3

1 Gray (1994a, p. 10).

2 For a detailed and comprehensive review of recent school effectiveness research see Sammons, Hillman and Mortimore (1995). See also Riddell and Brown (1991).

3 Mortimore (1991, p. 9).

4 Nottinghamshire's ambitious programme of research on pupil and school performance, for example, relies on multilevel modelling and is presented publicly as 'a value added analysis' (Farnsworth, Everett and Jesson, 1994).

5 Dearing (1994, p. 81, emphasis added).

6 SCAA (1994). For a critical commentary see Gray (1994b).

7 Reid, Hopkins and Holly (1987, p. 22).

8 Angus (1993, pp. 341-4).

9 See, for example, Thomas, Pan and Goldstein (1994).

10 Mortimore et al (1988).

11 Sammons (1994).

12 Later in this section we consider research on Lancashire (Thomas and Mortimore, 1994) and the AMA study (Thomas, Pan and Goldstein, 1994) which are among a small number of multilevel studies that include 'non-exam' pupils.

13 Bangladeshi pupils, for example, have frequently been among the groups entered for fewest examinations (Nuttall and Varlaam, 1990). Similarly, despite recent improvements, in Brent African Caribbean pupils are consistently entered for fewer exams than other groups (Brent, 1994).

14 Sammons (1994, p. 19).

15 Sammons (1994, p. 15, original emphasis).

16 Sammons (1994, p. 19, original emphasis).

17 Sammons (1994, pp. 29-30).

18 According to figures released in 1995, and drawn from the 1994 Labour Force Survey, just over one in three 'black' men in London (34 per cent) and one in five black women (22 per cent) are unemployed. For black young men, aged between 16 and 24, the figure is 62 per cent, i.e. more than three times the rate for white young men (20 per cent) in the same age group (Bevins and Nelson, 1995; Coleman, 1995).

19 According to estimates from the Spring 1994 Labour Force Survey, 'in the 16-24 age group, 51 per cent of young black men, 33 per cent of Bangladeshi men and 30 per cent of Indian men were unemployed compared with 18 per cent of white men' (Runnymede Trust, 1995b, p. 7).

20 Maughan and Rutter (1986); Mabey (1986); Kysel (1988).

21 Drew and Gray (1991).

22 Eggleston *et al* (1986), Tomlinson (1987).

23 Commission for Racial Equality (1992b), Gillborn (1990), Troyna and Siraj-Blatchford (1993), Wright (1986).

24 Smith and Tomlinson, 1989. For a critical discussion of the study, and media interpretations of its findings, see Gillborn and Drew (1992).

25 Smith and Tomlinson (1989, p. 266).

26 Smith and Tomlinson (1989, p. 32).

27 Thomas and Mortimore (1994, pp. 14-15).

28 Thomas, Pan and Goldstein (1994, pp. 10-11).

29 Thomas, Pan and Goldstein (1994, p. 10).

30 See Angus (1993) for an account of the historical background to school effectiveness research.

31 Thomas, Pan and Goldstein (1994, p. 7).

32 Thomas, Pan and Goldstein (1994, p. 7, original emphasis).

33 Thomas, Sammons and Mortimore (1994, p. 15).

34 Goldstein, Rasbash, Yang, Woodhouse, Pan, Nuttall and Thomas (1993, p. 431).

35 Thomas, Pan and Goldstein (1994, p. 8).

36 Mortimore, Sammons and Thomas (1994, p. 327).

37 Smith and Tomlinson (1989, p. 281).

38 Nuttall, Goldstein, Prosser and Rasbash (1989).

39 Drew and Gray (1991, p. 170).

40 Nuttall, Goldstein, Prosser and Rasbash (1989, p. 776).

41 Nuttall, Goldstein, Prosser and Rasbash (1989, p. 776).

42 Willms (1992, p. 41) quoted by Mortimore, Sammons and Thomas (1994, p. 328).

43 Sammons, Thomas, Mortimore, Owen and Pennell (1994, p. 34). See also Thrupp (1995).

44 Mortimore, Sammons and Thomas (1994, p. 328). For examples of compositional effects related to attainment see Nuttall and Varlaam (1990), Smith and Tomlinson (1989) and Willms (1985).

45 Mortimore, Sammons and Thomas (1994, p. 328). For examples of compositional effects related to poverty and measures of social class background see Nuttall and Varlaam (1990) and Sammons, Thomas, Mortimore, Owen and Pennell (1994).

46 See Nuttall and Varlaam (1990, p. 21).

47 Smith and Tomlinson (1989, p. 279).

4 Behind the numbers: qualitative research in multi-ethnic schools

Talk of achievement in education is dominated by statistics: as we have shown, however, quantitative approaches cannot supply all the answers - they tell us little about how certain patterns come to emerge. Looking inside schools and classrooms, to understand people's views of themselves and others, and to observe the daily life of institutions can help us to understand more about young people's attempts to achieve, and the processes that shape schooling: this is the aim of qualitative research. In many ways this approach offers a more penetrating perspective, revealing processes and experiences that may be hidden from quantitative measures: the incidence and nature of racial harassment and exclusion from school offer examples of this.

In this section we review the major findings that relate to the school experiences of African Caribbean and South Asian pupils and look to the future by considering how qualitative research might help us better to understand, and support, school change that improves the opportunities to succeed for all pupils.

4.1 QUALITATIVE RESEARCH: a different perspective?

It has been argued that 'Quantitative methods can only report *what* is happening; qualitative look at the *why* and the *how*'[1]: this has far reaching consequences for the style of research, the kinds of question that are addressed and the findings that emerge. This approach stresses the importance of understanding how teachers and pupils view their situation, what they expect of others and how they come together during the routine interactions that shape school life. A concern with *interaction* is especially important; two participants often see the same situation in different ways - their interaction might have consequences of which neither are fully aware.

One of the most distinctive aspects of qualitative research is the detail with which real life situations can be reported and analysed.

Such research can be both striking and insightful, raising unexpected questions and highlighting the importance of events and assumptions that may previously have been taken for granted.

This is especially true of 'ethnographic' research - a form of extended qualitative study where a single institution is researched in great detail, usually over a long time period (possibly a year or more)[2]. This involves certain limitations.

First, *there is a trade off between the detail with which institutions can be researched and the number of 'cases' that can be included:* it is common for qualitative researchers to examine a single school, usually focusing on a relatively small group of teachers and pupils.

Second, *interview and observational data are open to multiple interpretations.* Researchers usually combat this by presenting several different types of data to support their analyses: 'At best an ethnographer (like all social scientists) can only persuade the reader to agree that the explanation is a plausible one, but not that it is the *only* plausible one'[3]. Despite these weaknesses, qualitative research frequently offers a more revealing perspective, highlighting patterns of experience and achievement that are not visible in quantitative studies.

It is only comparatively recently that detailed qualitative studies have focused on multi-ethnic schools[4]. Since the publication of the Swann report, for example, several researchers have studied schools in the primary[5] and secondary sectors[6]. In this section we review some of these studies and, in view of the limitations we have noted, indicate how they might offer lines of interpretation to inform policy and practice.

Racial violence and harassment

The incidence of bullying and violence in schools is notoriously difficult to research: indeed, it is an issue where qualitative and quantitative approaches frequently produce markedly different findings. A survey of 18 multi-ethnic comprehensives, for example, found 'little indication of overt racism in relations among pupils'[7]; and yet a simultaneous ethnographic study of one of the same schools found that 'racist attacks (usually, but not always, verbal) were a regular fact of life for most Asian pupils'[8]. The different findings probably result from several factors; a questionnaire can only probe harassment in relatively crude ways, whereas qualitative researchers can see it first hand and build relationships of trust with pupils so that both aggressor and victim feel able to discuss their feelings and experiences.

In addition to the *frequency* of harassment inside the researched schools, qualitative approaches also offer a more textured understanding of the *nature* of the attacks. Accounts of classroom interaction and quotations from pupils help to illustrate the hurt and anger caused by *name calling* which might be viewed by adults as rather trivial.

- Qualitative studies illustrate that harassment, whether verbal or physical, is not always recognized as such by teachers, who may interpret such conflicts as simple boisterousness.

Additionally, qualitative studies suggest that racist harassment is influenced by a variety of stereotypes:

- Pupils of minority background do not appear to suffer harassment in equal measure; the most common victims are usually South Asian pupils.

This picture is consistent across studies of primary schools in the late 1980s[9] and early 1990s[10], and secondary schools from the 1970s[11] to late 1980s[12]. Research suggests that the combined influence of ethnic and gender stereotypes is an important factor; white pupils often view Asian peers as weaker and more vulnerable than African Caribbeans: Asian girls and young women, in particular, are subject to a range of, sometimes contradictory, racial and sexual stereotypes[13].

Qualitative work has played an important role in helping to reveal the extent and nature of racial harassment in a range of schools. Because of the limited number of case studies, however, it is not possible to judge from this research whether racial harassment has become more or less common in recent years. At a national level reliable statistics on this are no less difficult to collect and interpret[14]. Nevertheless, available data suggest that in recent years both the frequency of attacks and the sense of threat and insecurity has risen for South Asians[15]. A number of incidents have made national headlines; some are catalogued in Figure 4.1. It is important to remember, however, that *for each incident that reaches the headlines there are likely to be countless other 'lower level' attacks that go unreported*. Each incident 'affects not only the victim, and not only his or her family and close friends, but ... also contributes to a sense of threat, intimidation and insecurity for all members of the ethnic group to which the victim belongs'[16].

Exclusions from school

A second area where qualitative work might offer valuable insights is exclusion from school. Here statistics can do little more than highlight the problem; qualitative research may offer the best way of understanding how it arises.

Officially, exclusions should be used 'as a last resort rather than as a normal sanction for bad behaviour'[17]. Schools may exclude a pupil for a *fixed period* (say one or two days) or, in the most extreme cases, the exclusion may be *permanent* - in which case the pupil cannot return to that school and alternative arrangements must be made by the LEA. Permanent exclusion can have enormously detrimental effects on a young person's educational prospects. The most recent overall figures from the DfEE, for example, suggest that *two out of every three pupils who are permanently excluded never return to another mainstream school*[18]. Newly published research suggests that the figures for secondary pupils may be worse than this: of those permanently excluded in 1993-94, four out of every five failed to return to a mainstream school[19].

Figure 4.1

A brief chronology of racial violence against children and young people

1991

February: Rolan Adams, a 15-year-old black grammar school pupil from south London, is stabbed to death by a young neo-Nazi on the Thamesmead estate.

1992

July: Rohit Duggal, a 16-year-old Asian pupil, is stabbed to death during a confrontation with a group of white youths in Greenwich, south London.

October: Gangs of white and Asian youths involved in violent clashes outside Shawlands Academy, Glasgow.

1993

April: Black sixth-former Stephen Lawrence, 18, is stabbed to death by half a dozen white youths.

April: 14-year-old black Sheffield boy bayonets Grant Jackson, a 17-year-old white boy, to death during inter-school gang warfare.

May: Two Bengali youths, aged 17, are attacked with a machete by a skinhead as they sit on a wall outside one of their homes in Camden, north London.

September: Quaddus Ali, a 17-year-old Bangladeshi student at Tower Hamlets College, east London, is savagely beaten by a group of white men, including skinheads.

September: At least nine pupils transfer from George Green's School on the Isle of Dogs, Tower Hamlets, because of racial harassment.

1994

February: Muktar Ahmed, 19, savagely beaten by a gang of 20 white youths in Bethnal Green, east London. A few days later, a group of white youths armed with iron bars and accompanied by dogs attack Asian students sitting in a park during their lunch break from Tower Hamlets College. The following day a 14-year-old Bengali boy is stabbed in the face by four white men as he walks down Bethnal Green Road.

March: Violent clashes take place between black and Asian youths, some of them armed, in and around Quintin Kynaston School in St John's Wood, north London.

June: Student Shah Mohammed Ruhul Alam, 17, is critically wounded after being stabbed by 10 white youths.

August: Richard Everitt, a 15-year-old white pupil, is stabbed to death by a group of 11 Asian youths near King's Cross Station, north London.

December: The National Union of Students launches a 24-hour hotline to tackle growing harassment and intimidation of students by far-Right groups.

Source: Adapted from *Times Educational Supplement*, 6 January 1995, p. 9.

Quantitative material, gathered by a range of official bodies (most notably the DfEE and various LEAs) has clearly established an ethnic difference in exclusion rates:

- black young people are proportionately more likely to be excluded than members of other ethnic groups.

Exclusions, therefore, currently have a much greater impact on black young people. The only published national statistics for which an ethnic breakdown is available relate to permanent exclusions between 1990 and 1992: these suggest that four times as many African Caribbeans were being excluded than would be predicted given their numbers in the school population. Similar patterns emerge in more recent data from individual LEAs:

- black over-representation in exclusions is a widespread problem, affecting both primary and secondary schools[20].

Most permanent exclusions involve secondary age pupils and more boys are excluded than girls - by a ratio of around four to one in secondary schools[21]. These patterns hold true for black pupils, but *the relative over-representation of black girls (in comparison with other girls) can be at least as great as the figure for their male counterparts;* in one London borough, for example, African Caribbean girls accounted for almost twice the predicted number of secondary exclusions and around four times the expected level in primaries[22].

There are no definitive statistics on the current rate of exclusion nationally, but there are strong indications that the sanction is being used more frequently than ever before: a recent survey suggests that during the early 1990s, the number of permanent exclusions tripled over a three year period (to more than 10,000 per annum)[23]. Evidence gathered during OFSTED inspections in 1993-94 (summarized in Figure 4.2) provides probably the most reliable ethnic breakdown to date[24]:

- Black pupils (classified separately as Black African, Black Caribbean and Black Other) are the most frequently excluded.
- The figure for Black Caribbean young people is the worst; almost six times the rate of exclusion for whites.

These data are especially important, because they refer to a large and up-to-date sample of schools - between 25 and 30 per cent of all secondary schools in England.

The over-representation of black young people in exclusions is too large and consistent (over time and across regions) to be discounted as a statistical artefact or chance occurrence. However, existing research tells us little about the kinds of process that lie behind the exclusion statistics.

Officially, permanent exclusion is appropriate where 'allowing the child to remain in school would be seriously detrimental to the education or welfare of the pupil, or to that of others at the school'[25]. However, national information indicates that permanent exclusions are used for a much wider range of offences than originally intended:

• In the early 1990s, 'Disobedience in various forms - constantly refusing to comply with school rules, verbal abuse or insolence to teachers - was the major reason for exclusion.' [26]

Figure 4.2

Exclusions from secondary school by ethnic origin. England (1993-4)

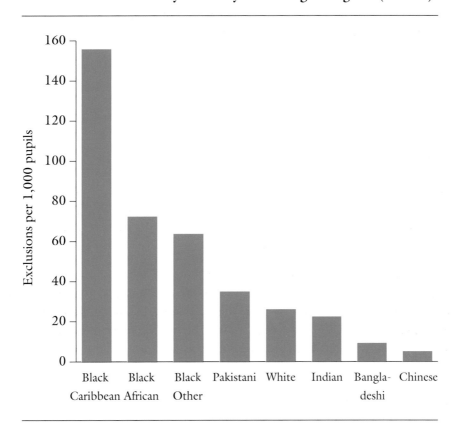

Source: OFSTED

Qualitative research (relying mostly on interviews with excluded pupils and their families) suggests that the sanction is sometimes used in an insensitive and hasty way; ethnic minority pupils, for example, have complained of discrimination against them on religious grounds or because they are assumed to represent a disciplinary challenge[27]. Unfortunately, to date, no detailed qualitative studies have been published that explore how exclusions fit within the life of schools, how they are viewed by teachers and headteachers, and the processes that lead some pupils to permanent exclusion while others remain in school or return after a temporary exclusion.

The rise in exclusions, and the disproportionate number of black pupils involved, have prompted a number of suggestions about the underlying factors: theories include reference to a supposed deterioration in discipline; the possibility of schools seeking to massage their achievement rates by removing certain pupils from the statistics; the impact of changing family structures; and even diet[28]. So far there is little research to help us judge which factors might be most significant. Existing qualitative studies suggest that conflict between teachers and pupils can differ according to pupils' ethnic origin. This may suggest one way in which the routine processes of schooling can have the unintended result of denying all pupils an equal opportunity to achieve.

4.2 ETHNIC ORIGIN AND TEACHER/PUPIL INTERACTIONS

It has long been recognised that one of the most important factors underlying academic achievement is the support and encouragement of knowledgeable and committed teachers; it is perhaps not surprising, therefore, that the nature of the interaction between teachers and ethnic minority pupils has been a common theme in most qualitative studies of multi-ethnic schools.

African Caribbean pupils

- Qualitative research frequently points to a relatively high level of tension, even conflict, between white teachers and African Caribbean pupils.

This emerged in one of the first detailed studies of a multi-ethnic school (a secondary modern studied in the early 1970s) and was repeated a decade later in research on two comprehensive schools[29]. Both researchers found that African Caribbean pupils were disciplined by teachers more often than other ethnic groups. Additionally, the more recent study described a situation where it was 'not uncommon' for teachers to blame black pupils for a perceived decline in standards of achievement; in both schools teachers complained of 'troublesome' black pupils[30]. Both researchers argued that the teacher/pupil conflict frequently arose from the way teachers dealt with black pupils; the earlier report talked of teachers' 'confusion' when faced with unfamiliar cultural styles, while the later project described a 'stimulus-response' situation where pupils identified and responded to expectations of low ability and disruptive behaviour[31].

A more detailed study, also conducted during the early 1980s, examined teacher/pupil relations in a boys' comprehensive and a co-educational sixth-form college[32]. As with the earlier studies, this project noted the deeply felt conflict between white teachers and black pupils; but it went further in exploring the *range* of teachers' perspectives and expectations, including positive attempts to improve black pupils' access to the curriculum. Here many teachers (even those who considered themselves 'liberal' and committed to equality of opportunity) operated with negative views of black pupils as disadvantaged by broken homes and pathological family structures[33]. This research also identified the range of racial stereotypes current in the boys' school:

- Despite their shared position as 'minorities', African Caribbean and Asian pupils can be subject to different expectations.

The researcher noted 'There was a tendency for Asian male students to be seen by the teachers as technically of "high ability" and socially as conformist. Afro-Caribbean male students tended to be seen as having "low ability" and potential discipline problems'[34].

Similarly, a study conducted in the mid-eighties in 'City Road Comprehensive' (a co-educational 11-16 school in the midlands) also found that African Caribbean pupils were 'in trouble' with teachers more frequently than any other ethnic group. Teachers often complained that black pupils displayed a 'bad attitude'; they were more likely to be criticized in class and more likely to be kept behind after school as punishment[35]. And yet City Road teachers, unlike those reported in previous studies, did not speak about the school in terms that suggested black pupils were responsible for any fall in standards. Indeed, during two years of fieldwork the majority of teachers seemed genuinely to be committed to the goal of equality of opportunity: some younger teachers had deliberately chosen the school because they wanted to teach in the inner city. Nevertheless, observations, interviews with pupils (of all ethnic backgrounds) and an analysis of school punishment records each suggested that, as a group, black pupils (of both sexes) were disproportionately criticized and disciplined by white teachers. For the African Caribbean pupils, teacher/pupil interaction was fraught with conflict and suspicion. Subsequent research, conducted in the late 1980s and early 1990s, in multi-ethnic primary and middle schools reports strikingly similar processes of heightened criticism and control[36].

To date, therefore, ethnographic research has revealed a high degree of conflict between black pupils and white teachers. Irrespective of the teachers' conscious desire to help all pupils equally, the level of teacher/pupil conflict in the researched schools was such that, as a group, black pupils experienced school in ways that were significantly more conflictual and less positive than their peers regardless of 'ability' and gender: the patterns were true for black pupils of both sexes and included some whom teachers described as having excellent academic potential. In the researched schools, therefore:

- Qualitative approaches reveal a considerable gulf between the daily reality experienced by many black pupils and the stated goal of equal opportunities for all.

If the patterns reported in these studies are repeated more widely, the consequences for the achievement of African Caribbean pupils are potentially very great. However, all researchers are not agreed on the factors at work in these schools.

Although qualitative studies typically reveal that black pupils are criticized significantly more often than their peers of other ethnic origins, this finding is open to many different, and contrasting, interpretations. It might be argued, for example, that as a group black pupils simply break school rules more often than their peers. This is the explanation offered by one researcher whose study of a northern comprehensive school in the mid-eighties found that when pupils were selected for hierarchical teaching groups ('sets') black young men were least likely to win a place in high status groups; 'a number of students who were defined as "bright enough" were ruled out because of their record of past behaviour ... these students were nearly all Afro/Caribbean boys'[37]. Here the researcher regarded the teachers' actions as reasonable and has gone on to criticize other researchers for seeming to 'victimise teachers' without having 'proven' that teacher racism is widespread[38].

As we have noted, absolute proof is not possible in social science research, and is especially difficult in relation to qualitative studies which, by their nature, focus on a small number of schools. Perhaps most importantly, such criticisms misinterpret the focus of qualitative research; the aim is not to *blame* anyone, but to understand the complex dynamics of teaching and learning:

> • Teachers (in their daily interactions with pupils) and schools (through the adoption of various selection and setting procedures) may play an active, though unintended, role in the creation of conflict with African Caribbean pupils, thereby reducing black young people's opportunity to achieve.

The study of 'City Road Comprehensive', for example, tried to make sense of the apparent contradiction between the teachers' good intentions and the reality of their differential treatment of black pupils; the research describes this as the working out of a complex and multifaceted series of constraints and stereotypes. The teachers believed that black pupils, as a group, presented a greater threat to classroom order and their personal safety. They 'expected' trouble from black pupils, sometimes perceived a threat where none was intended, and reacted quickly (as they saw it) to prevent further challenges.

From the pupils' perspective this meant that if several pupils were engaged in the same behaviour - say, talking during lessons - typically it would be a black pupil (rather than a white or Asian peer involved in the same discussion) who would be told to be quiet or moved to a different seat. Additionally, there was evidence of black pupils being criticized for behaviour which, although it broke no school rule, was interpreted as signifying arrogance or a poor attitude[39]. Consequently, despite their best intentions some teachers came unwittingly to create patterns of control that heightened conflict with African Caribbean pupils.

By focusing on the *consequences* of interaction in this way, qualitative research has begun to explore how racism might operate in ways that are more subtle and widespread than the crude, often violent, attitudes usually associated with notions of discrimination and prejudice. Although the research describes only a small number of schools in detail, its wider importance may lie in suggesting ways that practitioners could examine the assumptions and practices that shape the school experiences and achievements of their own pupils.

South Asian pupils

Although pupils of South Asian ethnic background are more numerous than their African Caribbean peers they have received much less attention in qualitative research. Nevertheless, research has begun to explore the complex lived experiences of Asian pupils. We have noted, for example, that the schools studied to date suggest:

> • Teachers often view Asian pupils as being better behaved, more highly motivated and of relatively higher ability in comparison with African Caribbean pupils[40].

However, it is also the case that *South Asian pupils can be subject to negative stereotypes which close down educational opportunities.* Problems with *language* have sometimes been misinterpreted as indicative of deeper seated *learning* difficulties, with the result that Asian pupils have been placed in inappropriate teaching groups or simply left out of the normal routine of classroom life[41]. Several qualitative studies have noted a common stereotype where it is assumed that Asian communities are excessively authoritarian; emphasizing narrow, restrictive expectations for their children, who are raised in families dominated by the rule of the father. Consequently:

- Negative stereotypes about Asian communities can lead to lower expectations for Asian pupils.

This appears to be especially so for young women, because it is believed that their future lives will be restricted by early marriage and the demands of the home[42].

This is a complex area, where reliable data on parental expectations are scarce. Interviews with 55 young Muslim women, predominantly of Pakistani background, indicated that around a third of their parents were unequivocally opposed to their daughters pursuing higher education[43]. Research on Punjabi Sikhs in the UK, however, shows that extended education for young women is actively encouraged by parents, and is supported by community norms that place a premium on women's education[44]. In addition, in comparison with white young women, the rates of participation in full time post compulsory education are greater for females in each of the major Asian groups. *Stereotypes of a lack of support for the education of young Asian women seem at best gross exaggerations and at worst untrue -* depending on specific cultural and local factors[45]. Additionally, research suggests that the view of Asians as relatively well behaved may be carried to further extremes in some teachers' treatment of Asian young women. Here a stereotype of passivity, of the 'docile' Asian girl, 'has often meant that the girls are systematically forgotten or ignored when it comes to demands on the teachers' time'[46].

The stereotype of South Asian communities as rigid, traditional and authoritarian, does not necessarily have the same consequences in all contexts.

- Ethnographic research suggests that Asian pupils' school experiences may vary according to the ethnic composition of their schools.

Where black pupils made up a significant proportion of the school population, research has suggested that teachers' expectations of Asians can be relatively positive. In contrast to their African Caribbean peers, Asians were assumed to benefit from family support and a settled home life that complemented the aims of the school. Where Asians were the dominant or sole ethnic minority group, however, there was evidence that (in the absence of black pupils) the same basic image of Asian communities emerged in different - more negative - forms. Here their actions could be seen as 'sly' rather than studious and the home community viewed as oppressive rather than supportive[47]. It must be remembered, however, that because of the small number of available studies, this analysis remains speculative.

Qualitative work in this field has tended to concentrate on the problems faced by ethnic minority pupils; however, we have already shown that some minority pupils achieve excellent results. These two findings are not inconsistent. Although qualitative work has given less attention to successful pupils, existing research suggests that the manner in which pupils adapt, in order to succeed, highlights similar problems to those faced by their less academically successful counterparts. Additionally, some qualitative research has begun to explore ways in which schools can change to improve pupils' experiences and raise levels of achievement.

High achieving ethnic minority pupils

In examining differences in achievement between pupils of the same ethnic origin, most qualitative researchers have concentrated on how pupils perceive and respond to their experiences in school. Where Asian pupils feature in the analyses qualitative work suggests that their responses to school reflect the importance of numerous factors, including past achievement, social class background, gender and their perceptions of racism in the school and beyond[48]. Research with black young people, on the other hand, is more consistent in its representation of ethnicity and gender as the most significant factors.

In view of the negative expectations often faced by African Caribbean pupils in the researched schools, it is perhaps not surprising that the qualitative literature provides several examples of pupils responding in negative terms by rejecting school. The notion of *resistance* is especially prominent - usually portraying some pupils' 'anti-school' positions as a response to racism[49]. However, *a rejection of others' negative expectations does not necessarily entail a rejection of school and education in its entirety.*

Some researchers describe the actions of black pupils who, while refusing to accept others' negative evaluations of them, nevertheless remain committed to academic success. Studies of African Caribbean young women, in particular, provide evidence of pupils seeing academic success as a means of ensuring their own independence after school and fighting stereotypes in constructive (rather than self-defeating) ways[50]:

- Pupils' responses do not necessarily divide simply between rejection (resistance) and accommodation (conformity): some pupils creatively combine elements of both resistance and conformity.

Studies of academically successful African Caribbean young men are comparatively rare[51]:

- A combination of gender and racial stereotypes may make it more difficult for black young men to avoid being caught up in cycles of increasingly severe criticism and control.

Whereas African Caribbean girls are often described as 'boisterous' and 'noisy', it is their male peers who are typically seen as presenting the most serious threat to teachers' authority and who are likely to experience more severe sanctions within school. Regardless of gender, however, it is clear that for black pupils academic success brings additional challenges and sacrifices: case studies of successful black pupils frequently highlight the personal costs involved in accommodating to others' expectations, sometimes at the expense of criticism from their peers[52].

Changing Schools

Qualitative research has begun to examine how multi-ethnic schools have attempted to change their ethos, curriculum and management styles, so as to improve the experiences and achievements of pupils, regardless of ethnic background. The research shows that where teachers, pupils, parents and local communities are genuinely involved in developments, important changes can be introduced on a whole-school basis (not simply in isolated project or topic work). The studies demonstrate the long, unpredictable, often painful, nature of school change, especially where teachers and pupils begin seriously to consider experiences and viewpoints they may previously have taken for granted. Research in secondary schools suggests that small 'core' groups of staff may be necessary to provide the impetus for change; in infant and primary schools the teaching staff may be small enough to allow whole-school developments to occur at an earlier stage[53]. Despite differences in the schools that have been researched, some common findings have emerged:

- Without backing from the headteacher and/or other senior members of staff, widespread change is unlikely;

- Teachers, ancillary and care staff all have vital roles to play and should be included in programmes of inservice education that are sensitive to the complexity of the issues and build a sense of shared involvement[54];

- Making genuine links with local communities and involving parents can be exceptionally difficult, but appears to be a key factor in supporting and extending successful change[55];

- The most successful work has been characterized by a concern actively to involve pupils in devising and implementing policy changes.

Despite the limitations of small case study research, qualitative work can offer a unique perspective on many crucial issues through the depth of understanding and detail that it produces. To date, the majority of work in this field has concentrated on the problems facing ethnic minority pupils and not on their successes. In the future, it is possible that similar research methods will help develop a more sensitive and perceptive basis for attempts to improve the educational experiences and achievements of all pupils.

1 Gordon (1984, p. 106) quoted by Troyna (1993, p. 100, emphasis added).

2 Some writers have begun to use 'ethnography' as another term for any form of qualitative research, including short-term interview based projects. More specifically, however, ethnographic studies are usually characterised by long periods 'in the field' and often make use of multiple forms of data. See Burgess (1984).

3 Brewer (1994, p. 243, original emphasis).

4 Writing in the late 1980s, for example, Paul Atkinson and his colleagues (Atkinson, Delamont and Hammersley, 1988) were only able to cite a handful of qualitative projects concerned with the experiences of ethnic minority pupils; including Driver (1979), Fuller (1980) and Furlong (1984).

5 Connolly (1995), Epstein (1993), Troyna and Hatcher (1992) and Wright (1992).

6 Foster (1990), Gillborn (1990), Mac an Ghaill (1988), Mirza (1992) and Wright (1986).

7 Smith and Tomlinson (1989, p. 63).

8 Gillborn (1990, p. 78).

9 Wright (1992).

10 Connolly (1995).

11 Willis (1977).

12 Gillborn (1990).

13 See Brah (1992).

14 See Runnymede Trust (1994), Skellington with Morris (1992) and Virdee (1995).

15 Runnymede Trust (1994, pp. 28-9).

16 Runnymede Trust (1994, p. 28). See also Virdee (1995).

17 DFE (1993, p. 2).

18 DFE (1993, p. 4).

19 Responses from 101 LEAs (92 per cent of all LEAs) indicate that in 1993/94 the 'return to mainstream school appears to be accomplished for 27% of primary pupils but for only 15% of secondary pupils' (Parsons, 1995, para. 5.3). The report's author feels these figures are likely to under-estimate the true level, 'possibly by as much as 25%': even so, this would mean a return rate of less than one in five secondary pupils.

20 See Bourne, Bridges and Searle (1994), Cohen and Hughes (1994) and Gillborn (1995, Ch. 2).

21 Parsons (1995, para. 4.5) and DFE (1993, p. 4). In primary schools the ratio of excluded boys to girls is much higher, 12 boys to every girl permanently excluded in 1993/94 (Parsons, 1995, para. 4.5).

22 Source: Lewisham Education Committee (1993).

23 The National Exclusions Reporting System identified 2,910 permanent exclusions in 1990/91. The most comprehensive recent survey (including more than 90 per cent of all LEAs) found 10,624 permanent exclusions in 1993/94. The same report estimates a total national figure of 11,181 (Parsons, 1995, para. 4.7 and Table 3).

24 These data include all types of exclusion. To control for differences in the total size of ethnic groups, the OFSTED data are calculated as a rate of exclusion per 1,000 pupils. In 1993-94 the white rate was 27.07 per 1,000 pupils. The rate for Black Caribbeans was 156.09; Black African 72.66; Black Other 63.20. The rates for South Asian pupils do not vary dramatically from the white figure, with the exception of Bangladeshis who - like Chinese pupils - are markedly under-represented: Indian 22.40; Pakistani 34.50, Bangladeshi 9.05, Chinese 5.13 per 1,000 pupils. Source: OFSTED.

25 DFE (1994, para. 5).

26 DFE (1992, p. 3).

27 For examples from interviews and case records see Blair (1994) and Bourne, Bridges and Searle (1994).

28 See, for example, the Elton report (1989, pp. 163-4).

29 Driver (1977 and 1979) and Wright (1986).

30 See Wright (1986, p. 130). The Swann report includes a section on Peter Green's classroom observation research (Swann, 1985, pp. 46-56). Green's work describes the frequency of different teacher/pupil interactions but gives no sense of their flavour or meaning.

31 Driver (1979) and Wright (1986, p. 130-46).

32 Mac an Ghaill (1988).

33 See Mac an Ghaill (1988, Ch. 2). For a discussion of racist stereotypes and the reality of African Caribbean families from the perspective of black young women see Mirza (1992).

34 Mac an Ghaill (1988, p. 64).

35 Gillborn (1990, see especially Ch. 2). Note that 'City Road Comprehensive' is a false name - in order to protect the people who took part in the research, qualitative studies usually disguise the true identity of the institutions that were researched.

36 See Wright (1992) and Connolly (1995).

37 Foster (1990, p. 143).

38 Foster (1993, p.550) and (1991, p. 165). For more detailed discussion of Foster's work see Gillborn (1995, Ch. 3) and Hammersley (1995, Ch. 4).

39 See Gillborn (1990) and Wright (1992) for examples from lesson observations and tape recorded interviews.

40 See Gillborn (1990) and Mac an Ghaill (1988; 1989).

41 Troyna and Siraj-Blatchford (1993) and Wright (1992).

42 See Gillborn (1990), Mac an Ghaill (1988; 1989) Shepherd (1987) and Wright (1992).

43 Brah and Shaw (1992, p. 43).

44 Bhachu (1985).

45 Gibson and Bhachu (1988).

46 Brah and Minhas (1985, p. 19).

47 Gillborn (1992), Mac an Ghaill (1989) and Shepherd (1987).

48 See Gillborn (1990) and Mac an Ghaill (1988; 1989).

49 See for example, Wright (1986) and Mac an Ghaill's description of a group of African Caribbean boys, 'The Rasta Heads' (Mac an Ghaill, 1988, Ch. 3).

50 See, for example, Fuller (1980), Mac an Ghaill (1988; 1989) and Mirza (1992).

51 See Gillborn (1990, pp. 60-70).

52 See Mac an Ghaill (1988) and Mirza (1992).

53 Epstein (1993), Gillborn (1995) and Siraj-Blatchford (1994).

54 The changing status of race and ethnicity within teacher education is examined by Gaine (1995, Ch. 7). See also Deshpande and Rashid (1993) and Verma (1993).

55 It is vital that schools try to involve all sections of their feeder communities; work on racism and equal opportunities, for example, may have divisive and counter-productive results where the white community is not seen as an important partner: see Macdonald, Bhavnani, Khan and John (1989) and Vincent (1995).

5 Post Compulsory education

This section discusses research on participation in education beyond the end of compulsory schooling. It has been known for some time that, in comparison with their white counterparts, young people from ethnic minority backgrounds tend to 'stay on' in full time education more often; we examine this trend and evidence that certain minority groups may be unfairly treated in their attempts to enter high status institutions.

5.1 'STAYING ON': educational participation between 16 and 19

The number of young people 'staying on' in education beyond the statutory requirement has been rising continuously in Britain since the mid- to late-1980s[1].

- A majority of young people now remain in full time education following their compulsory schooling.

This dramatic development reflects several factors; among the most important are the increase in GCSE achievements (described earlier) and the changing economic situation, especially as it affects the youth labour market: 'Employers are not just recruiting less youth labour: recruiting practices and the occupational structure of the youth labour market have changed as well. There are now significantly fewer jobs for school leavers. Figure 5.1 shows how rising staying on rates contrast with a fall in youth employment: between 1989 and 1992, the proportion of 16-17 year olds in full time work halved.'

Improvements in average GCSE performance over recent years is thought to account for just over half the increase in full time participation; however, staying on has also become more popular among those with 'average and below average GCSE results'[4]. This, combined with the traditionally higher staying on rates for young people from middle class backgrounds, means that those from relatively advantaged class backgrounds are now likely to remain in education whatever their GCSE results[5].

Figure 5.1

16-17 year olds in full time education or full time work (1989-92)

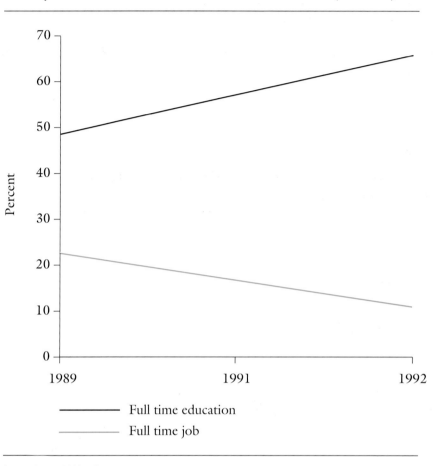

Source: Payne, 1995, p.3

Ethnic origin and post compulsory participation

At the time of the Swann report (1985) it was already known that young people from ethnic minority backgrounds tended to remain in education more often than their white counterparts[6]. It was not until the early 1990s, however, that research on a large and nationally representative sample began to unpack some of the complexities of the situation. Drawing on a sample of more than 28,000 16-year-olds in 1985 and 1986, David Drew and his colleagues state:

- 'once attainment was taken into account, ethnic origin was the single most important variable in determining the chances of staying on'[7].

When other factors (such as achievement at 16, social class, gender and parental education) were taken into account, the differences between ethnic group participation became particularly striking: 'other things being equal, the odds of Afro-Caribbeans staying on were three times higher than for whites; and for Asians they were ten times higher than for whites'[8].

Fewer young people remain in full time education with each year that passes after the age of 16. Nevertheless, *the differences between ethnic group participation rates remain clear throughout the first three post-compulsory years*[9] (see Figure 5.2). The higher participation rate for Asian young people is especially notable:

- A majority of Asians are still in full-time education three years after the end of their compulsory schooling.

Figure 5.2

Participation rates in full time education by ethnic origin and post compulsory year

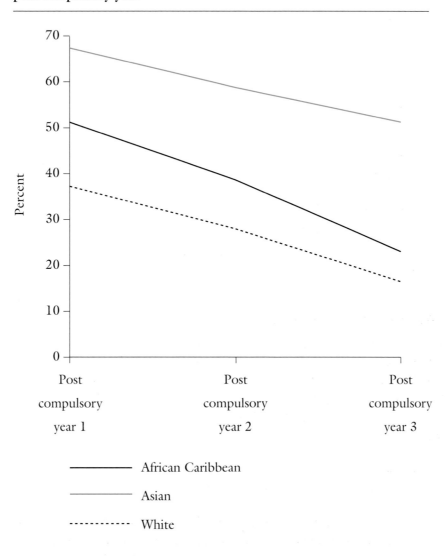

Source: Adapted from Drew, Gray and Sime, 1992, p.7.

The census provides a more detailed snap-shot of post compulsory participation and allows comparison between different social class backgrounds. Figure 5.3 shows that *within each ethnic group*, the higher the social class background, the higher the rate of post compulsory participation. However, clear differences remain between ethnic groups:

> • In almost every case, minority pupils are more likely to stay on than whites from the same social class[10].

In fact, the differences between ethnic groups are so large that *in some cases young people of minority ethnic origin from lower social class backgrounds are more likely to stay on than whites from a higher socio-economic group* [11]. The census data suggest that a crude tripartite ethnic division (White, Asian and African Caribbean) over-simplifies the situation. The major South Asian groups (Indian, Pakistani, Bangladeshi) continue to participate in full time education at consistently high levels. It is the Black African group, however, that stays on most often among young people from skilled and semi- or un-skilled backgrounds.

Gender differences are also reflected in staying on rates. *Young women tend to stay on more often than young men* (see Figure 5.4). In 1991, the overall rates were 47 per cent of females and 42 per cent of males[12]. However, *this pattern does not hold for all ethnic minority groups: staying on is more common among young men in each of the largest South Asian communities* [13]. This fact should be interpreted with caution: although a common stereotype paints South Asian women as especially powerless and suffering restricted opportunities because of community traditions[14], *the proportion of white young women who stay in full time education is less than the figure for every major ethnic minority group.*

The greater staying on rates among ethnic minority young people are clear and consistent. However, research cannot yet offer any conclusive explanations for these patterns. Three possible reasons are most commonly offered:

> • *Motivation and parental support:* it may be that minority communities have a greater commitment to education and value qualifications more highly. Certainly young people from minority backgrounds report more parental encouragement to remain in education[15].
>
> • *Unemployment:* young people of minority background frequently experience higher rates of unemployment. In these circumstances staying on may appear to be the best option, either as a way of postponing entry into the labour market or, more positively, in the hope of up-grading educational certification[16].
>
> • *Resisting racism:* pupils of ethnic minority background often place a special value on educational qualifications as a way of demonstrating their qualities in the basic currency of competition for educational and job opportunities[17]. However, even within further and higher education, racism is experienced by some black and Asian students[18].

Figure 5.3

Participation rates of 16-19 year olds in full time education by social class and ethnic origin (1991)

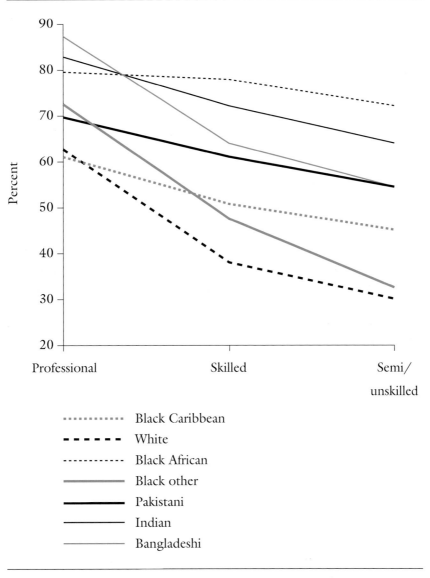

Source: Drew, Gray and Sporton, 1994, table 2.2.

Ethnic origin and courses of study in post compulsory education

Further education offers a wide range of courses and levels of study, which differ in their status and marketability as credentials. The highest status is generally accorded to the familiar and established academic route, characterised by studying toward Advanced (A) level qualifications[19]. Not surprisingly, the type of course studied in post compulsory education is strongly associated with differences in achievement at 16:

Figure 5.4

Participation rates of 16-19 year olds in full time education by gender and ethnic origin (1991)

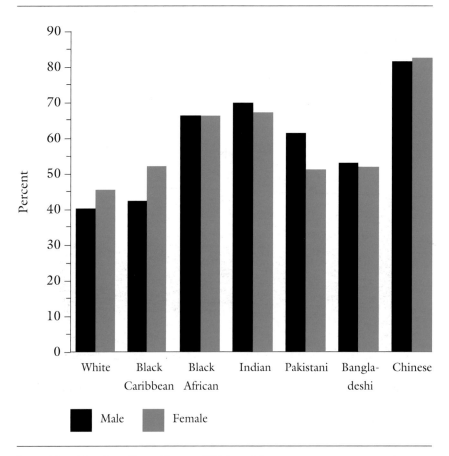

Source: Adapted from Drew, Gray and Sporton, 1994, figure 2.3.

> • Virtually all students with high GCSE attainments were on GCE A-level/AS courses ... the proportion on these courses fell rapidly as GCSE results got poorer, and the proportion doing GCSE courses increased. The proportion doing vocational courses only was also greatest amongst those with poor GCSE results, and fell sharply amongst students with five or more GCSE A-C grades[20].

Lack of up-to-date research makes it difficult to be certain how different ethnic groups are represented in the different paths through further education. The best available data relate to young people who reached the end of compulsory schooling in 1985 and 1986[21]. Having completed three years of post compulsory education by the start of the 1990s, many of these young people will by now have graduated from university.

Figures 5.5, 5.6 and 5.7 show the courses followed by White, Asian and African Caribbean young people still in full time education one, two and three years after they could have left school aged 16[22]. The figures suggest several important trends:

Figure 5.5

Course participation during three years of full time post compulsory (PC) education: white young people

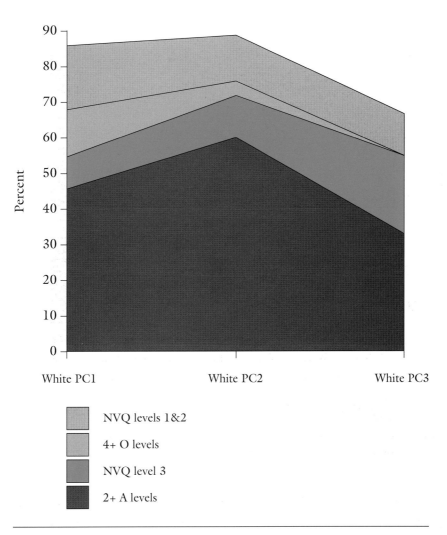

Source: Adapted from Drew, Gray and Sime, 1992, table 2.6.

- White and Asian young people are more likely to follow the traditional 'academic' route of two or more A level courses.

- Among Asian young people, there is a particular emphasis on taking 'O' levels (now GCSEs) in the first post compulsory year (almost a third of those still in education), then transferring to 'A' level courses.

- In comparison, African Caribbean young people are more likely to take vocational qualifications.

Figure 5.6

Course participation during three years of full time post compulsory (PC) education: Asian young people

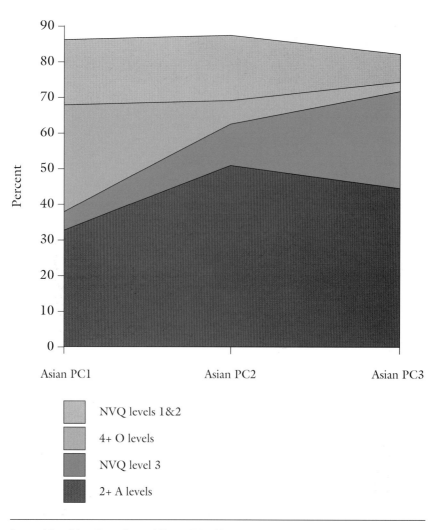

Source: Adapted from Drew, Gray and Sime, 1992, table 2.6.

Although both Asian and African Caribbean young people stay in full time education more frequently than whites, their resulting profile of qualifications is somewhat different. *By the age of 18 Asian young people are the most highly qualified group,* placing them in a relatively strong position for entry into higher education. For African Caribbean young people, their relatively lower achievements at age 16 continue to have ramifications; they are more likely to study vocational courses in further education and (despite emerging as the best vocationally qualified group) they may not be well placed in the competition for access to university.

Figure 5.7

Course participation during three years of full time post compulsory (PC) education: African Caribbean young people

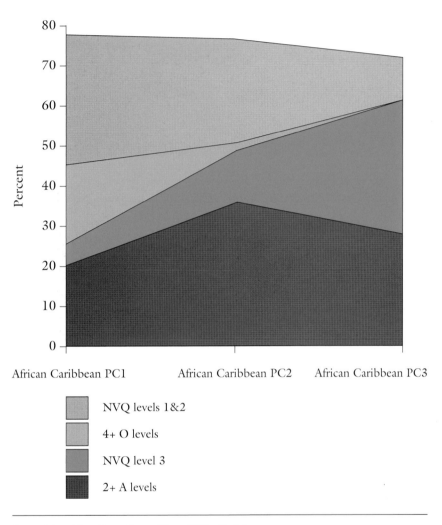

Source: Adapted from Drew, Gray and Sime, 1992, table 2.6.

Higher education (HE) has seen important changes in recent years, notably the removal of the division between universities and polytechnics (the so-called 'binary line'). Applicants to higher education now approach their chosen institutions through the Universities and Colleges Admissions Service (UCAS): prior to these changes two separate bodies were involved; the Universities Central Council on Admissions (UCCA) and the Polytechnic Central Admissions System (PCAS). Data gathered by the admissions systems offer a means of examining ethnic minority representation in attempts to gain *access* to HE. Unfortunately, there is still no parallel system for monitoring the subsequent *achievement* of minority students. Research in a small number of HE institutions in the north of England suggests that a higher proportion of African Caribbean students dropped out before their final examinations, but the sample was not representative and should be viewed with extreme caution[23].

It is only recently that entry to higher education has been formally monitored for signs of possible discrimination against ethnic minority groups: PCAS introduced a question on applicants' ethnic origin in 1989, and this was adopted by UCCA a year later[24]. A major influence here was the discovery that a computer program, used to sort applications to a medical school, was systematically disadvantaging ethnic minority and female applicants[25]. The information on ethnic background collected by PCAS and UCCA provided the first opportunity to examine entry to higher education based on comprehensive data[26]. The first returns suggested that certain ethnic minority groups were rather more successful than others, and that overall 'minority ethnic groups are well represented among those entering HE relative to the general population'[27]. Unfortunately, early research did not examine the *interaction* of different factors that might influence applicants' chances of success (such as levels of certification, social class background, gender etc.). New research, by the Policy Studies Institute (PSI), begins to unravel these factors[28].

The PSI study worked with data from 1992 and so deals separately with university and polytechnic access. In comparison with their representation in the population:

> • Young people of minority background accounted for proportionately more *applications* to higher education (+56 per cent to universities and +86 per cent to polytechnics).

These proportions changed significantly, however, when considering *admissions:* ethnic minority 'over-representation' in universities fell (to +12 per cent of entrants), but rose in polytechnics (to +96 per cent)[29]. Table 5.1 summarises the major features of admissions analysed by ethnic group and type of HE institution.

> • Rates of admission vary considerably between different minority groups.

The PSI report notes that *the patterns cannot be described in terms of simple black/white or black/Asian/white divisions;* 'Asian and black groups were distributed both within the under-represented and over-represented groups'[30]. The authors' use of the phrases 'over-' and 'under-representation', however, should be viewed with caution at this stage. These calculations are based on raw figures - no allowance has been made for differences in qualifications; furthermore, the difference in status between universities and polytechnics was such that many applicants accepted offers of places in both systems, finally taking up the university place if they achieved sufficiently high A level scores. Admission to the two sets of institutions, therefore, did not operate in completely separate ways[31].

As Table 5.1 illustrates, there were significant differences between university and polytechnic admissions rates - only around one in four Black Africans entering higher education was admitted to university. A greater proportion of White applicants was accepted by universities than any other group, while the least successful were Black Caribbeans and Black Africans[32] (see Figure 5.8).

Table 5.1

Admissions to higher education by ethnic group and type of institution (1992)

Level of representation among admissions compared to the proportion of the 15-24 age group in Britain (Census, 1991).

CHINESE	OVER-represented in admissions to university	(+109%)
	OVER-represented in admissions to polytechnic	(+86%)
INDIAN	OVER-represented in admissions to university	(+19%)
	OVER-represented in admissions to polytechnic	(+91%)
BLACK AFRICAN	OVER-represented in admissions to university	(+14%)
	OVER-represented in admissions to polytechnic	(+243%)
BLACK CARIBBEAN	UNDER-represented in admissions to university	(-63%)
	OVER-represented in admissions to polytechnic	(+43%)
PAKISTANI	UNDER-represented in admissions to university	(-19%)
	OVER-represented in admissions to polytechnic	(+48%)
BANGLADESHI	UNDER-represented in admissions to university	(-45%)
	UNDER-represented in admissions to polytechnic	(-8%)
WHITE	UNDER-represented in admissions to university	(-1%)
	UNDER-represented in admissions to polytechnic	(-7.5%)

Source: Modood and Shiner, 1994, adapted from tables 1 & 2, pp. 2-3.

Note: The percentages should be interpreted as follows: Chinese people are over-represented in university admissions by 109 per cent, i.e. they are twice as likely to be admitted than their percentage in the 15-24 age group would suggest. In contrast, Black Caribbean representation in university admissions is 63 per cent lower than that which we would expect given the size of the 15-24 age group.

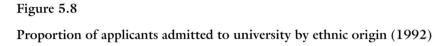

Figure 5.8

Proportion of applicants admitted to university by ethnic origin (1992)

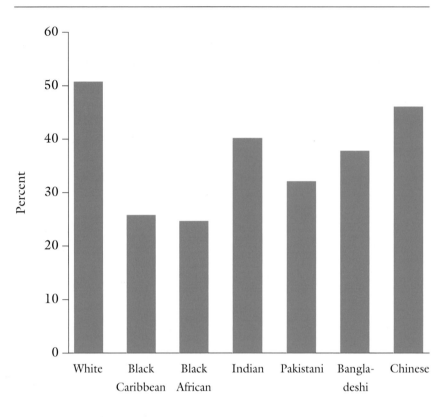

Source: Adapted from Modood and Shiner, 1994.

In an attempt to explain such discrepancies, UCCA highlighted a range of factors that might work against minority applicants[33]:

- Young people of minority background might face unusually fierce competition for places because relatively few apply for courses with low entrance requirements;

- Minority applicants are more likely to apply to institutions in their home region; UCCA suspected that this worked against them;

- As a group, minority applicants tend to be less well qualified, with lower A level scores and more qualifications gained through re-sits, which admissions officers might view less favourably.

By controlling for differences in achievement, social class and other background factors, the PSI study attempted to judge the validity of UCCA's suggestions. Not surprisingly, the report confirms that prior achievement is a hugely important factor in gaining admission to university. However, the report also found that, *all other things being equal, a range of background factors were associated with differences in admission:*

- *Gender:* men are more likely to be admitted to university than women;

- *School attended:* those who attend a selective school are more likely to be admitted than those who attend non-selective schools;

- *Social class:* applicants with parents in professional/managerial occupations are more likely to be admitted than those from skilled, semi- or un - skilled backgrounds;

- *Home region:* contrary to UCCA's expectations, those who apply to local universities are more likely to be accepted;

- *Age:* older applicants are more likely to be admitted to university than younger ones.[34]

These findings highlight inequalities operating at the entry point to higher education: regardless of their qualifications, young people from working class backgrounds who have attended non-selective schools appear to face particular barriers. These factors are likely to apply to a larger proportion of ethnic minority young people. However, even when these additional sources of inequality are taken into account, significant differences remain in rates of admission:

- 'Black Caribbean and Pakistani applicants continued to be significantly less likely to have been admitted to university;

- Chinese and Asian-other [i.e. excluding Indian, Pakistani & Bangladeshi] applicants continued to be significantly more likely to have gained admission to university.' [35]

In concluding their analysis of the 1992 UCCA and PCAS data, the PSI authors argue that despite the apparent injustices suffered by Caribbean and Pakistani applicants to university, the overall situation in the higher education sector may be more equitable because of the numbers of minority students entering polytechnics[36]. This is a useful observation, but we should be careful not to lose sight of the very real differences in status that are often accorded the 'old' universities over the 'new' ones (the old polytechnics). This could have significant knock-on effects when minority young people enter the graduate job market. Indeed, as competition for higher education places intensifies (as a result of the increase in staying-on rates), there is good cause to fear that increased selection might begin to operate to the disadvantage of certain minorities across the unified higher education sector.

NOTES TO SECTION 5

1 Drew, Gray and Sporton (1994, p.1). See also Spours (1995).

2 Payne (1995, p. iii).

3 Payne (1995, Table 1.1, p. 3).

4 Payne (1995, p. iii).

5 Payne (1995, p. iii).

6 Craft and Craft (1983).

7 Drew, Gray and Sime (1992, p. 12: emphasis added).

8 Drew, Gray and Sime (1992, p. 13).

9 Adapted from Drew, Gray and Sime (1992, Table 1.1, p. 7).

10 The only exception are 'Black Caribbeans' from professional backgrounds. Source: Drew, Gray and Sporton (1994, see Table 2.2): these figures relate to the 1991 census and are drawn from the 2 per cent individual sample of anonymised records.

11 Whites from professional backgrounds are less likely to stay on than Black Africans, Indians and Bangladeshis from skilled backgrounds. Similarly, skilled Whites are less likely to stay on than Black Caribbeans, Black Africans, Indians, Pakistanis and Bangladeshis from semi-skilled or un-skilled backgrounds: Drew, Gray and Sporton (1994, Table 2.2).

12 Drew, Gray and Sporton (1994, p. 3).

13 The largest male/female gap is for Pakistani young people (11 percentage points), the smallest is for Bangladeshis (1 per cent).

14 See, for example, Brah and Minhas (1985), Gillborn (1990, Ch. 4), Mac an Ghaill (1988, Ch. 1), Shepherd (1987).

15 In Drew's research 70 per cent of Asian, and 66 per cent of African Caribbean young people reported that their families had advised them to stay on: the figure for Whites was 48 per cent (Drew, Gray and Sime, 1992, Table 2.3, p. 11).

16 See Drew (1995).

17 See, for example, Mac an Ghaill (1988, pp. 26-35).

18 See Crozier and Menter (1993) and Mirza (1994).

19 Although less common, most research studies include Advanced Supplementary (AS) level courses in their A level calculations; see, for example, Modood and Shiner (1994, p. 9) and Payne (1995).

20 Payne (1995, p. 20).

21 Drew, Gray and Sime (1992).

22 Calculated using data in Drew, Gray and Sime (1992, Table 2.6, p. 15).

23 Skellington with Morris (1992, pp. 128-9) describe the 'preliminary findings' of research on students who entered HE 'without traditional qualifications'. The study is reported to indicate that more than 25 per cent of African Caribbeans did not take final examinations, compared with 15 per cent of Asians and 17 per cent of whites. Also African Caribbeans were less likely to receive degrees in the highest classifications (first or upper second class).

24 Taylor (1993, p. 427).

25 CRE (1988b).

26 Previous studies used more limited samples; typically focusing on a relatively small number of institutions or individuals: Taylor (1993, p. 426), for example, highlights the studies by Bird and colleagues (1992a & b), Lyon (1988), Singh (1990) and Tomlinson (1983).

27 Taylor (1993, p. 429).

28 Modood and Shiner (1994).

29 Modood and Shiner (1994, p. 4).

30 Modood and Shiner (1994, p. 4).

31 Because of this we have chosen to concentrate mainly on admissions to those institutions where competition was most severe, i.e. the (old) universities. For detail on the construction of the PSI samples see Modood and Shiner (1994, pp. 7-8).

32 Modood and Shiner (1994, p. 14).

33 UCCA (1991 and 1992) summarized by Modood and Shiner (1994, p. 5-6).

34 Modood and Shiner (1994, pp. 38-9).

35 Modood and Shiner (1994, p. 46).

36 Modood and Shiner (1994, p. 49).

6 Conclusions

In this review we have examined the most important recent research on the educational achievements and school experiences of ethnic minority pupils. We have focused almost exclusively on work published within the last ten years, much of it within the last five. Additionally we have analysed original material, from a range of LEAs, that supplements and extends the existing research base[1]. Many things have changed in the decade since the Swann Committee reported: among the many encouraging developments that our review highlights are:

- Generally higher levels of achievement, increasing year on year;

- Improving levels of attainment among ethnic minority groups in many areas of the country;

- Dramatic increases in the examination performance of certain minority groups, even in LEAs where there is significant poverty;

- In higher education, people of ethnic minority background are generally well represented among those continuing their education to degree level.

However, the review also illustrates the need for critical consideration of changes, keeping sight of the continuing differences in educational experience and achievement between certain groups. We have noted, for example:

- The gap is growing between the highest and lowest achieving ethnic groups in many LEAs;

- African Caribbean young people, especially boys, have not shared equally in the increasing rates of achievement; in some areas their performance has actually worsened;

- The sharp rise in the number of exclusions from school affects a disproportionately large number of black pupils;

- Even when differences in qualifications, social class and gender are taken into account, ethnic groups do not enjoy equal chances of success in their applications to enter university.

We hope that this review, by identifying trends and pointing to connections across different research traditions, will make a positive contribution to the advancement of work in this field. Nevertheless, as with any review, the overriding concern has been with the past. In this final section we turn to the future.

There are no simple answers to the range of educational issues raised by ethnic diversity. In reviewing previous research for this study, it has been necessary to recognise gaps in existing knowledge and failures in the past to learn from mistakes. This review charts the importance of ethnic origin as a factor in educational achievement from infant school to university. It is crucial that ethnicity is considered when new agendas are debated or targets set.

• Monitoring achievements and needs

Gathering reliable information about the experiences, achievements and needs of ethnic minority groups is increasingly seen as an essential part of improving standards for all. The DfEE recently outlined an important role for ethnic monitoring at the school, LEA and national level[2]. This is a sensitive and difficult area, where the co-operation of parents and pupils can be vital.

To repay the investment of time and resources it is essential, first, that monitoring exercises are sufficiently detailed to produce useful information and, second, that the results are used to good effect. The need for improvement in this area is clear; the existing Ethnic Monitoring Survey of School Pupils has failed consistently to produce meaningful and reliable data[3]. Recent OFSTED inspections report clear evidence of good ethnic monitoring in less than one school in every two hundred inspected[4]. The need for urgent action in this area could not be more clear.

• A focus on ethnicity

Ethnic diversity is not a 'cities-only' issue. The needs of minority pupils are neither uniform, nor simple. Sometimes explicitly targeted provision may be necessary: section 2 shows that focused support, such as that for language learning (usually funded by Section 11 resources) can have tangible benefits in terms of the achievement of bilingual pupils. Such work may be weakened by the insecurity of Section 11 posts and new budgetary arrangements that cannot ring-fence resources to ensure spending on bilingual support.

In addressing the standard of education provided by schools the government has given a major role to school inspections; OFSTED inspections could provide a major spur to increased attention in this field. Amendments to the *Framework for the Inspection of Schools,* for example, require inspection reports to comment where 'the educational standards achieved by particular groups of pupils vary unduly' - allied to a requirement to 'ensure that the full range of age, gender, ability, special educational need, and ethnic background is taken into account'[5]. Schools should be required to respond to any such issues and the publication of aggregated data from OFSTED inspections could significantly improve our understanding of provision across the country.

- **Achievement for all**

Many schools and LEAs have responded to the calls for improved standards by emphasizing the need to maximise achievement in external examinations, especially at GCSE. This response is hardly surprising given the high profile of the annual school performance tables. Nevertheless, while overall GCSE performance has risen, in many cases the gap has increased between the highest and lowest achieving groups. Similarly some schools are known to be more effective for high achieving pupils - possibly ensuring their success at the expense of peers who are perceived to be less able. Among ethnic minority groups, African Caribbean pupils may be affected by these processes more than most; in some LEAs, for example, it is not so much that black pupils are improving at a slower rate, rather that their average achievements are falling.

This is an issue of immediate concern; this review has demonstrated that *all* groups can improve their performance - strategies to raise achievement should also address the dangers of increasing the gaps between different groups by targeting those with different needs.

- **Ethnicity and the whole school**

Failure to address ethnic diversity has proved counter-productive at the school level. Where schools have adopted 'colour-blind' policies, for example, inequalities of opportunity have been seen to continue. In contrast, research has begun to examine the benefits of addressing diversity as an important and changing part of school life. In this country 'multi-culturalism' has received some support at a national level (though often marginal and focused mainly on the curriculum). The word 'anti-racism' has been applied rather loosely and, in many cases, its practical application at the school level is uncertain. Nevertheless, some local authorities and individual schools have worked seriously at developing practical and workable approaches to ethnic diversity. Research shows that the past has produced both failure and success and suggests there are no easy formulae, but a wide ranging attempt to address ethnicity is long overdue in many schools. It also suggests that, sensitively and self-critically handled, schools' approaches to multiculturalism and anti-racism can make a real impact; reducing racial harassment and involving pupils in genuine and supportive ways[6].

- **A Research Agenda**

Reviews of this sort reflect an assumption that research can have a positive effect by informing future policy and practice. The competition for research funding is now more intense than ever[7]: in these circumstances, it is useful to identify some of the gaps revealed by this review. A research agenda could be compiled around these gaps.

- **Teaching and Learning in multi-ethnic schools**

There are relatively few detailed studies of teaching and learning in multi-ethnic schools and colleges. A greater range of studies is needed to improve understanding of how ethnicity operates in a variety of contexts and in relation to the dimensions of social class and gender. Additionally, of course, many schools have significant ethnic minority populations from groups that are largely absent from previous research - such as Turkish and Greek pupils and those who have recently entered the country as refugees: how do they experience life in multi-ethnic schools? Research should include the different phases of education; cover different geographical regions; and include different school types.

• Successful multi-ethnic schools

In section 3 we discussed research showing that some secondary schools may be especially effective for certain minority groups. A whole series of questions immediately suggest themselves: can schools be effective for all ethnic groups? What factors make for effective multi-ethnic schools? Such research should not rely solely on quantitative approaches: section 4 shows how survey approaches can fail to penetrate the complex, sometimes hidden, processes that operate at the school and classroom level. Qualitative work has started to explore this area, a combination of ethnographic techniques with quantitative research offers the opportunity to examine these issues more fully.

• Understanding change and supporting improvement

This review has explored changing levels of achievement between, and within, ethnic groups. Many schools and LEAs are actively pursuing ways of raising pupils' achievements. Some of these projects have been successful, some have not. A good deal could be learnt from systematic examination of such work. We need to know what has been tried; why certain strategies are chosen in preference to others; which approaches have shown most signs of success; and how this can be explained?

• Exclusions from school

It seems essential that a co-ordinated response is launched to reduce the number of exclusions from school. In isolation, however, lowering the numbers (say, by changing the regulations) will not address the underlying reasons for the consistent over-representation of black pupils among those excluded. Most discussion of exclusions takes place away from school - excluded pupils and their families have been interviewed; statistics have been gathered and their interpretation debated. *Research so far has omitted any consideration of how exclusions fit into the life of schools.* Indeed, teachers' perspectives are absent from a good deal of the research altogether[8]. And yet, exclusions are the result of school-based processes: whatever the appeal to outside influences, exclusions represent a decision by the school (or parts of it) to remove a child from the roll. Further research on this issue at school level is a priority.

These issues are not exhaustive, but they suggest the basis for an important programme of research. It is necessary to remember, however, that ethnic origin is not the only relevant factor: in reviewing research on pupils' achievements we have stressed the need to keep sight of many issues (especially social class and gender) that interact with ethnicity. Additionally there are significant socio-historical influences which mean that data on particular regions should not be assumed to represent the national picture.

This review has highlighted the continued, and growing, significance of ethnic diversity in education. More pupils than ever before now gain high levels of educational achievement, although a disproportionate number of ethnic minority young people continue to achieve less well on average. We have traced some of these differences in detail and outlined some of the ways that future research, policy and practice might begin to address existing inequalities.

NOTES TO SECTION 6

1   Full details of our LEA sample and its rationale are included as an appendix.

2   DfEE (1995, p.1). See also CRE (1992a).

3   DfEE (1995, p.2 and appendix A).

4   From a total of more than 900 inspections in 1994/5, in only 4 schools was there clear evidence of good ethnic monitoring: source, OFSTED.

5   See DfEE (1995, p. 4) and OFSTED (1995, pp. 5-6).

6   See, for example, section 4 where we discuss work on change in multi-ethnic schools.

7   Gipps (1993).

8   We know of two projects that are currently exploring aspects of exclusion in primary and secondary schools. The date for publication of final reports, however, is not yet certain.

Appendix

Details of LEAs sampled for this research

The time involved in academic analysis and publication can sometimes create a considerable delay in research evidence becoming widely available. It is not unusual, for example, to find newly published studies based on examination results that are already several years old. In order to gather more up-to-date material, from a range of different localities, it was decided to approach individual LEAs.

Limits to time and resources meant that we could not approach every LEA in England. However, a 100 per cent sample is unnecessary in view of the largely urban nature of ethnic minority communities. By selecting LEAs in view of the size of minority populations (aged 5-15) it was possible to include sufficient authorities to cover each of the largest ethnic minority groups in the country. Additionally, we approached certain LEAs whom we knew to have embarked on new or interesting projects likely to address relevant issues of ethnicity and educational experience/performance.

Our final sample included 34 English LEAs:

Barnet	*Hackney*	*Lewisham*	*Southwark*
Bedfordshire	*Haringey*	*Manchester*	*Tower Hamlets*
Berkshire	*Harrow*	*Newham*	*Wakefield*
Birmingham	*Hounslow*	*Nottingham*	*Waltham Forest*
Bradford	*Islington*	*Oldham*	*Wandsworth*
Brent	*Kirklees*	*Oxford*	*Westminster, City of*
Camden	*Lambeth*	*Redbridge*	*Wolverhampton*
Croydon	*Lancashire*	*Rochdale*	
Ealing	*Leicestershire*	*Sandwell*	

These authorities serve more than half the total ethnic minority population of Britain. The sample covers a wide range of authorities, including Inner London, Outer London, Metropolitan districts and shire counties. For each of the principal ethnic groups (Indian, Pakistani, Bangladeshi, Black African, Afro-Caribbean) the ten most populous LEAs were included. Additionally, five of the top ten authorities for Chinese pupils also appear.

Bibliography

Angus, L. (1993) 'The sociology of school effectiveness', *British Journal of Sociology of Education*, 14(3): 333-45.

Atkinson, P., Delamont, S. and Hammersley, M. (1988) 'Qualitative research traditions: a British response to Jacob', *Review of Educational Research*, 58(2): 231-250.

Ball, S.J. (1987) *The Micro-Politics of the School: Towards a Theory of School Organization*. London, Methuen.

Ballard, R. and Kalra, V.S. (1994) *The Ethnic Dimensions of the 1991 Census: A Preliminary Report*. Manchester, University of Manchester.

Bevins, A. and Nelson, D. (1995) 'Blacks stranded at the back of the jobs queue', *The Observer*, 12 February, p. 5.

Becker, H.S. (1980) Unpublished interview with Jef Verhoeven.

Bhachu, P. (1985) *Twice Migrants: East African Sikh Settlers in Britain*. London, Tavistock.

Bird, J., Yee, W., Myler, A. (1992a) *Widening Access to Higher Education for Black People*. Bristol, Bristol Polytechnic.

Bird, J., Sheibani, A. and Francombe, D. (1992b) *Ethnic Monitoring and Admissions to Higher Education*. Bristol, Bristol Polytechnic.

Birmingham City Council (1994) *Report of the Chief Education Officer: Education Services Committee: National Curriculum Assessment 1994: Key Stage One Results*. Birmingham, Birmingham City Council.

Birmingham City Council (1995) *Report of the Chief Education Officer: Education Committee: 14th November 1995. Examination Results 1995*. Birmingham, Birmingham City Council.

Blair, M. (1994) 'Interviews with Black families'. In R. Cohen *et al* (1994) *op cit.*

Bourne, J., Bridges, L. and Searle, C. (1994) *Outcast England: How Schools Exclude Black Children*. London, Institute of Race Relations.

Bradford Education Department (1994) *1994 Examination Results: A Level Year 13, GCSE Year 11: Aggregated Analysis*. Bradford, Bradford Education Policy & Information Unit.

Brah, A. (1992) 'Women of South Asian origin in Britain: issues and concerns'. In P. Braham, A. Rattansi and R. Skellington (eds)(1992) *Racism and Antiracism: Inequalities, Opportunities and Policies*. London, Sage.

Brah, A. and Minhas, R. (1985) 'Structural racism or cultural difference: Schooling for Asian girls'. In G. Weiner (ed.) *Just a Bunch of Girls: Feminist Approaches to Schooling*. Milton Keynes, Open University Press.

Brah, A. and Shaw, S. (1992) *Working Choices: South Asian Young Muslim Women and the Labour Market*. Research paper no. 91. London, Department of Employment.

Brent (1994) *Report summarising the analysis of the 1993 GCSE results*. London, London Borough of Brent.

Brewer, J. (1994) 'The ethnographic critique of ethnography: sectarianism in the RUC', *Sociology*, 28(1): 231-44.

Brown, C. (1992) 'Racial inequality in the British labour market', *Employment Institute Economic Report*, 5(4).

Burgess, R.G. (1984) *In the Field: An Introduction to Field Research*. London, George Allen & Unwin.

Burgess, R.G. (ed.)(1985) *Strategies of Educational Research: Qualitative Methods.* Lewes, Falmer.

Byford, D. and Mortimore, P. (1985) *School Examination Results in the ILEA 1984. Report RS977/85.* London, Inner London Education Authority.

Camden (1995) *Analysis of 1994 London Reading Test and GCSE Results by Ethnic Group: Report of the Director of Education to the Education (Strategy) Sub-Committee.* London, London Borough of Camden.

Clough, E. and Drew, D. with Wojciechowski, T. (1985) *Futures in Black and White: Two Studies of the Experiences of Young People in Sheffield and Bradford.* Sheffield, Pavic Publications & Sheffield City Polytechnic.

Cohen, R. and Hughes, M. with Ashworth, L. and Blair, M. (1994) *School's Out: The Family Perspective on School Exclusion.* London, Family Service Units and Barnardo's.

Coleman, J. (1968) 'The concept of equality of educational opportunity', *Harvard Educational Review*, special issue, 38(1): 7-22. Reprinted in B.R. Cosin, I.R. Dale, G.M. Esland, D. Mackinnon and D.F. Swift (eds)(1971) *School and Society: A Sociological Reader.* London, Routledge and Kegan Paul.

Coleman, P.K. (1995) 'Out of touch in towers of glass and steel', *The Runnymede Bulletin*, 283, pp. 8-9.

Commission for Racial Equality (1988a) 'Ethnic classification system recommended by CRE', *Press Statement.* London, Commission for Racial Equality.

Commission for Racial Equality (1988b) *Investigation into St George's Hospital Medical School.* London, Commission for Racial Equality.

Commission for Racial Equality (1992a) *Ethnic Monitoring in Education.* London, Commission for Racial Equality.

Commission for Racial Equality (1992b) *Set to Fail? Setting and Banding in Secondary Schools.* London, Commission for Racial Equality.

Connolly, P. (1995) 'Racism, masculine peer-group relations and the schooling of African/Caribbean infant boys', *British Journal of Sociology of Education*, 16(1): 75-92.

Craft, M. and Craft, A. (1983) 'The participation of ethnic minority pupils in further and higher education', *Educational Research*, 25(1): 10-19.

Crozier, G. and Menter, I. (1993) 'The heart of the matter? Student teachers' experiences in school'. In I. Siraj-Blatchford (ed.) *'Race', Gender and the Education of Teachers.* Buckingham, Open University Press.

Dearing, R. (1994) *The National Curriculum and its Assessment: Final Report.* London, School Curriculum and Assessment Authority.

Delamont, S. (1990) *Sex Roles in the School.* 2nd edn. London, Routledge.

Demaine, J. (1989) 'Race, categorisation and educational achievement', *British Journal of Sociology of Education*, 10(2): 195-214.

Department for Education (1992) *Exclusions: A Discussion Document.* London, DFE.

Department for Education (1993) 'A new deal for "out of school" pupils - Forth', *DFE News.* 126/93, 23 April.

Department for Education (1994) *Exclusions from School. Circular no. 10/94.* London, DFE.

Department for Education (1995) *Ethnic Monitoring of School Pupils: A Consultation Paper.* London, DFE.

Deshpande, P. and Rashid, N. (1993) 'Developing equality through Local Education Authority INSET'. In I. Siraj-Blatchford (ed.) *'Race', Gender and the Education of Teachers*. Buckingham, Open University Press.

Douglas, J.W.B. (1964) *The Home and the School*. London, McGibbon & Kee.

Drew, D. (1995) *'Race', Education and Work: The Statistics of Inequality*. Aldershot, Avebury.

Drew, D. and Fosam, B. (1994) 'Gender and ethnic differences in education and the youth labour market: a statistical review'. Paper presented at the annual meeting of the British Sociological Association, March.

Drew, D., Fosam, B. and Gillborn, D. (1995) 'Race, IQ and the underclass: don't believe the hype', *Radical Statistics*, 60: 2-21.

Drew, D. and Gray, J. (1990) 'The fifth year examination achievements of Black young people in England and Wales', *Educational Research*, 32(3): 107-117.

Drew, D. and Gray, J. (1991) 'The Black-White gap in examination results: a statistical critique of a decade's research', *New Community*, 17(2): 159-72.

Drew, D., Gray, J. and Sime, N. (1992) *Against the Odds: The Education and Labour Market Experiences of Black Young People. England & Wales Youth Cohort Study, Report R&D No. 68*. Sheffield, Employment Department.

Drew, D., Gray, J. and Sporton, D. (1994) 'Ethnic Differences in the Educational Participation of 16-19 Year Olds'. Unpublished paper presented to the OPCS/ESRC Census Analysis Group Conference, University of Leeds, September.

Driver, G. (1977) 'Cultural competence, social power and school achievement: West Indian secondary school pupils in the West Midlands', *New Community*, 5(4): 353-9.

Driver, G. (1979) 'Classroom stress and school achievement: West Indian adolescents and their teachers'. In V. Saifullah Khan (ed) *Minority Families in Britain: Support and Stress*. London, Macmillan, pp. 131-44.

Eggleston, S.J., Dunn, D.K. and Anjali, M. (1986) *Education for Some: The Educational & Vocational Experiences of 15-18 year old Members of Minority Ethnic Groups*. Stoke-on-Trent, Trentham.

Elton, R. (1989) *Discipline in Schools: Report of the Committee of Enquiry chaired by Lord Elton*. London, HMSO.

Epstein, D. (1993) *Changing Classroom Cultures: Anti-Racism, Politics and Schools*. Stoke-on-Trent, Trentham.

ENCA (1992) Shorrocks, D., Daniels, S., Frobisher, L., Nelson, N., Waterson, A. and Bell, J. *The Evaluation of National Curriculum Assessment at Key Stage 1, Final Report*. Leeds, University of Leeds School of Education.

Farnsworth, S., Everett, S. and Jesson, D. (1994) *Beyond League Tables: A Value-Added Analysis of GCSE and A level Performance in Nottinghamshire in 1993*. Nottingham, Nottinghamshire County Council.

Foster, P. (1990) *Policy and Practice in Multicultural and Anti-Racist Education*. London, Routledge.

Foster, P. (1991) 'Case still not proven: a reply to Cecile Wright', *British Educational Research Journal*, 17(2): 165-70.

Foster, P. (1993) ' "Methodological purism" or "a defence against hype"? Critical readership in research in "race" and education', *New Community*, 19(3): 547-52.

Fuller, M. (1980) 'Black girls in a London comprehensive school'. In M. Hammersley and P. Woods (eds)(1984) *Life in School: The Sociology of Pupil Culture*. Milton Keynes, Open University Press, pp. 77-88.

Furlong, V.J. (1984) 'Black resistance in the liberal comprehensive'. In S. Delamont (ed) *Readings on Interaction in the Classroom.* London, Methuen, pp. 212-236.

Gaine, C. (1995) *Still No Problem Here.* Stoke-on-Trent, Trentham.

Gibson, M.A. and Bhachu, P.K. (1988) 'Ethnicity and school performance: a comparative study of South Asian pupils in Britain and America', *Ethnic and Racial Studies,* 11(3): 239-262.

Gillborn, D. (1990) *'Race', Ethnicity & Education: Teaching and Learning in Multi-Ethnic Schools.* London, Unwin-Hyman/Routledge.

Gillborn, D. (1992) 'Racism and education: issues for research and practice'. In S. Brown and S. Riddell (eds) *Class, Race and Gender in Schools: A New Agenda for Policy and Practice in Scottish Education.* Edinburgh, Scottish Council for Research in Education with the Educational Institute of Scotland.

Gillborn, D. (1995) *Racism and Antiracism in Real Schools: theory . policy . practice.* Buckingham, Open University Press.

Gillborn, D. and Drew, D. (1992) ' "Race", class and school effects', *New Community,* 18(4): 551-65.

Gipps, C. (1993) 'The profession of educational research', *British Educational Research Journal,* 19(1): 3-16.

Gipps, C. and Murphy, P. (1994) *A Fair Test? Assessment, Achievement and Equity.* Buckingham, Open University Press.

Goldstein, H. (1987) *Multi-level Models in Social and Educational Research.* London, Griffin Press.

Goldstein, H., Rasbash, J., Yang, M., Woodhouse, G., Pan, H., Nuttall, D. and Thomas, S. (1993) 'A multilevel analysis of school examination results', *Oxford Review of Education,* 19(4): 425-33.

Gordon, L. (1984) 'Paul Willis - education, cultural production and social reproduction', *British Journal of Sociology of Education,* 5: 105-16.

Gould, S.J. (1981) *The Mismeasure of Man.* New York, W.W. Norton.

Gray, J. (1994a) 'Iterating the not necessarily obvious', *Times Educational Supplement,* 9 December, pp. 10-11.

Gray, J. (1994b) 'Relative values', *Times Educational Supplement,* 15 December, p. 15.

Gray, J. and Jesson, D. (1989) *Education and Training Opportunities in the Inner City. England & Wales Youth Cohort Study: Report RD51.* Sheffield, Employment Department.

Green, P.A. (1985) 'Multi-ethnic teaching and the pupils' self-concepts'. In the Swann Report, *Education for All: Final Report of the Committee of Inquiry into the Education of Children from Ethnic Minority Groups.* London, HMSO, pp. 46-56.

Halsey, A.H., Heath, A.F. and Ridge, J.M. (1980) *Origins and Destinations: Family, Class, and Education in Modern Britain.* Oxford, Clarendon Press.

Hammersley, M. (1995) *The Politics of Social Research.* London, Sage.

Hammersley, M. and Atkinson, P. (1995) *Ethnography: Principles in Practice.* Second edition. London, Routledge.

Herrnstein, R.J. and Murray, C. (1994) *The Bell Curve: Intelligence and Class Structure in American Life.* New York, Free Press.

Home Office (1981) *Racial Attacks.* London, HMSO.

Inner London Education Authority (1990) *Differences in Examination Performance.* London, ILEA Research & Statistics Branch.

Kamin, L.J. (1974) *The Science and Politics of IQ.* Harmondsworth, Penguin.

Kysel, F. (1988) 'Ethnic background and examination results', *Educational Research*, 30(2): 83-9.

Lambeth (1994) *Summer 1993 Examination Achievement at GCSE: Report by the Director of Education*. London, London Borough of Lambeth.

Lewisham Education Committee (1993) *Education Statistics Bulletin 1991-1992*. London, Lewisham Education.

Lyon, E. (1988) 'Unequal opportunities: Black minorities and access to Higher Education', *Journal of Further and Higher Education*, 12(3): 21-37.

Mabey, C. (1986) 'Black pupils' achievements in Inner London', *Educational Research*, 28(3): 163-73.

Mac an Ghaill, M. (1988) *Young, Gifted and Black: Student- Teacher Relations in the Schooling of Black Youth*. Milton Keynes, Open University Press.

Mac an Ghaill, M. (1989) 'Coming-of-age in 1980s England: reconceptualising Black students' schooling experience', *British Journal of Sociology of Education*, 10(3): 273-86.

Macdonald, I., Bhavnani, R., Khan, L. and John, G. (1989) *Murder in the Playground: The Burnage Report*. London, Longsight.

Mason, D. (1995) *Race and Ethnicity in Modern Britain*. Oxford, Oxford University Press.

Maughan, B. and Rutter, M. (1986) 'Black pupils' progress in secondary schools: II. Examination achievements', *British Journal of Developmental Psychology*, 4(1): 19-29.

Measor, L. and Sikes, P. (1992) *Gender and Schools*. London, Cassell.

Mirza, H.S. (1992) *Young, Female and Black*. London, Routledge.

Mirza, H.S. (1994) 'Black students in higher education: a movement for change'. Paper presented at the Society for Research in Higher Education annual conference, University of York, December.

Modood, T. (1992) *Not Easy Being British: Colour, Culture and Citizenship*. Stoke-on-Trent, Runnymede Trust and Trentham Books.

Modood, T., Beishon, S. and Virdee, S. (1994) *Changing Ethnic Identities*. London, Policy Studies Institute.

Modood, T. and Shiner, M. (1994) *Ethnic Minorities and Higher Education: Why are there differential rates of entry?* London, Policy Studies Institute.

Mortimore, P. (1991) 'The nature and findings of research on school effectiveness in the primary sector'. In S. Riddell and S. Brown (eds) *op cit*.

Mortimore, P., Sammons, P., Stoll, L., Lewis, D. and Ecob, R. (1988) *School Matters: the Junior Years*. Wells, Open Books.

Mortimore, P., Sammons, P. and Thomas, S. (1994) 'School effectiveness and value added measures', *Assessment in Education*, 1(3): 315-332.

Nottinghamshire County Council (1993) *Key Stage 1: A Commentary on the 1992 Assessments in Nottinghamshire*. Nottingham, Nottinghamshire County Council.

Nuttall, D.L., Goldstein, H., Prosser, R. and Rasbash, J. (1989) 'Differential school effectiveness', *International Journal of Educational Research*, 13: 769-76.

Nuttall, D. and Varlaam, A. (1990) *Differences in Examination Performance. RS 1277/90*. London, Inner London Education Authority Research and Statistics Branch.

Office for Standards in Education (1995) *New Framework for the Inspection of Schools: Draft for Consultation.* London, OFSTED.

Parsons, C. (1995) *Final Report to the Department for Education: National survey of local education authorities' policies and procedures for the identification of, and provision for, children who are out of school by reason of exclusion or otherwise.* London, DFE.

Payne, J. (1995) *Routes Beyond Compulsory Schooling. England and Wales Youth Cohort Study Report no. 31.* Sheffield, Employment Department.

Plewis, I. (1991) 'Pupils' progress in reading and mathematics during primary school: associations with ethnic group and sex', *Educational Research,* 33(2): 133-40.

Plewis, I. and Veltman, M. (1994) *Where does all the time go? Changes in infant pupils' experiences since the Education Reform Act.* London, University of London Institute of Education.

Rampton, A. (1981) *West Indian Children in Our Schools. Cmnd 8273.* London, HMSO.

Reid, I. (1989) *Social Class Differences in Britain: Life-Chances and Life-Styles.* 3rd edn. London, Fontana.

Reid, K., Hopkins, D. and Holly, P. (1987) *Towards the Effective School.* Oxford, Blackwell.

Richardson, R. (1994) 'The underclass in our times', *The Runnymede Bulletin,* no. 280, November, pp. 2-3.

Riddell, S. (1992) *Gender and the Politics of the Curriculum.* London, Routledge.

Riddell, S. and Brown, S. (1991) *School Effectiveness Research: Its Messages for School Improvement.* Edinburgh, HMSO.

Runnymede Trust (1994) *Multi-Ethnic Britain: Facts and Trends.* London, Runnymede Trust.

Runnymede Trust (1995a) *Challenge, Change and Opportunity: Overview, Texts and Agenda.* London, Runnymede Trust.

Runnymede Trust (1995b) *The Runnymede Bulletin,* no. 286, June.

Rutter, M., Maughan, B., Mortimore, P. and Ouston, J. with Smith, A. (1979) *Fifteen Thousand Hours: Secondary Schools and their Effects on Children.* Shepton Mallet, Open Books.

Sammons, P. (1994) 'Gender, ethnic and socio-economic differences in attainment and progress: a longitudinal analysis of student achievement over nine years'. Paper prepared for the symposium 'Equity Issues in Performance Assessment', Annual meeting of the American Educational Research Association, New Orleans, April.

Sammons, P., Hillman, J. and Mortimore, P. (1995) *Key Characteristics of Effective Schools: A Review of School Effectiveness Research.* London, University of London Institute of Education.

Sammons, P., Thomas, S., Mortimore, P., Owen, C. and Pennell, H. (1994) *Assessing School Effectiveness: Developing Measures to put School Performance in Context.* London, University of London Institute of Education.

School Curriculum and Assessment Authority (1994) *Value-Added Performance Indicators for Schools.* London, School Curriculum and Assessment Authority.

Shepherd, D. (1987) 'The accomplishment of divergence', *British Journal of Sociology of Education,* 8(3): 263-76.

Siraj-Blatchford, I. (1994) *The Early Years: Laying the Foundations for Racial Equality.* Stoke-on-Trent, Trentham.

Singh, R. (1990) 'Ethnic minority experience in Higher Education', *Higher Education Quarterly,* 44(4): 344-359.

Skellington, R. with Morris, P. (1992) *'Race' in Britain Today.* London, Sage.

Smith, D.J. and Tomlinson, S. (1989) *The School Effect: A Study of Multi-Racial Comprehensives.* London, Policy Studies Institute.

Southwark (1994) *Education Statistics 1993-94.* London, London Borough of Southwark.

Spours, K. (1995) *Post-16 Participation, Attainment and Progress.* London, University of London Institute of Education.

Strauss, A. (1987) *Qualitative Analysis for Social Scientists.* Cambridge, Cambridge University Press.

Swann, Lord (1985) *Education for All: Final Report of the Committee of Inquiry into the Education of Children from Ethnic Minority Groups.* Cmnd 9453. London, HMSO.

Tattum, D. (ed.)(1993) *Understanding and Managing Bullying.* Oxford, Heinemann.

Taylor, P. (1993) 'Minority ethnic groups and gender in access to Higher Education', *New Community,* 19(3): 425-40.

Thomas, S. and Mortimore, P. (1994) *Report on Value Added Analysis of 1993 GCSE Examination Results in Lancashire.* London, University of London Institute of Education.

Thomas, S., Pan, H. and Goldstein, H. (1994) *Report on the Analysis of 1992 Examination Results: AMA Project on Putting Examination Results in Context.* London, Association of Metropolitan Authorities.

Thomas, S., Sammons, P. and Mortimore, P. (1994) 'Stability and Consistency in Secondary Schools' Effects on Students' GCSE Outcomes'. Paper presented at the annual conference of the British Educational Research Association, Oxford, September.

Thrupp, M. (1995) 'The school mix effect: the history of an enduring problem in educational research, policy and practice', *British Journal of Sociology of Education,* 16(2): 183-203.

Tizard, B., Blatchford, P., Burke, J., Farquhar, C. and Plewis, I. (1988) *Young Children at School in the Inner City.* Hove, Lawrence Erlbaum.

Tizard, B. and Phoenix, A. (1993) *Black, White or Mixed Race? Race and Racism in the Lives of Young People of Mixed Parentage.* London, Routledge.

Tomlinson, S. (1983) 'Black Women in Higher Education - Case Studies of University Women in Britain'. In L. Barton and S. Walker (eds) *Race and Class in Education.* London, Croom Helm.

Tomlinson, S. (1987) 'Curriculum option choices in multi-ethnic schools'. In B. Troyna (ed.) *Racial Inequality in Education.* London, Tavistock.

Tomlinson, S. (1992) 'Disadvantaging the disadvantaged: Bangladeshis and education in Tower Hamlets', *British Journal of Sociology of Education,* 13(4): 437-46.

Tower Hamlets (1994) *Analysis of 1994 GCSE Results.* London, London Borough of Tower Hamlets.

Troyna, B. (1984) 'Fact or artefact? The "educational underachievement" of black pupils', *British Journal of Sociology of Education,* 5(2): 153-66.

Troyna, B. (1993) *Racism and Education: Research Perspectives.* Buckingham, Open University Press.

Troyna, B. and Hatcher, R. (1992) *Racism in Children's Lives: A Study of Mainly White Primary Schools.* London, Routledge.

Troyna, B. and Siraj-Blatchford, I. (1993) 'Providing support or denying access? The experiences of students designated as "ESL" and "SN" in a multi-ethnic secondary school', *Educational Review*, 45(1): 3-11.

UCCA (1991) *Statistical Supplement to the twenty-eighth Report, 1989-1990*. Cheltenham, UCCA.

UCCA (1992) *Statistical Supplement to the Twenty-ninth Report, 1990-1991*. Cheltenham, UCCA.

Verhoeven, J. (1989) *Methodological and Metascientific Problems in Symbolic Interactionism*. Leuven, Departement Sociologie, Katholieke Universiteit Leuven.

Verma, G. (ed.)(1993) *Inequality and Teacher Education*. Lewes, Falmer.

Vincent, C. (1995) 'School, community and ethnic minority parents'. In S. Tomlinson and M. Craft (eds) *Ethnic Relations and Schooling*. London, Athlone.

Virdee, S. (1995) *Racial Violence and Harassment*. London, Policy Studies Institute.

Wandsworth Education Department (1992) *Ethnic Monitoring and Pupil Achievement in Wandsworth Schools. Research Report REU 22/92*. London, London Borough of Wandsworth.

Wandsworth Education Department (1993) *Wandsworth Baseline Assessment 1992/93. Research Report REU 31.93*. London, London Borough of Wandsworth.

Wandsworth Education Department (1994a) *Key Stage 1 Assessment Results. Research Report REU 44.94*. London, London Borough of Wandsworth.

Wandsworth Education Department (1994b) *Wandsworth Assessment Programme: Year 6 Test Results 1993/94. Research Report REU 40.94*. London, London Borough of Wandsworth.

Wandsworth Education Department (1995) *Wandsworth Baseline Assessment 1994/95. Research Report REU 46/95*. London, London Borough of Wandsworth.

Willis, P. (1977) *Learning to Labour: How Working Class Kids Get Working Class Jobs*. Farnborough, Gower.

Willms, J.D. (1985) 'The balance thesis - contextual effects of ability on pupils "O" grade examination results', *Oxford Review of Education*, 11: 33-41.

Willms, J.D. (1992) *Monitoring School Performance: A Guide for Educators*. London, Falmer.

Wilson, A. (1987) *Mixed Race Children: A Study of Identity*. London, Allen & Unwin.

Wright, C. (1986) 'School processes - an ethnographic study'. In J. Eggleston, D. Dunn and M. Anjali (1986) *Education for Some: The Educational & Vocational Experiences of 15-18 year old Members of Minority Ethnic Groups*. Stoke-on-Trent, Trentham.

Wright, C. (1992) *Race Relations in the Primary School*. London, David Fulton Publishers.

Printed in the United Kingdom for HMSO
Dd 302691   C40   7/96